PBS
Tier 1 Manual

A Knowledge-Outcomes Impact Model for Multi-Tiered Systems of Behavioural Support

4th Edition

International Edition 1.4

Daniel Gulchak, Ph.D.,

Yadira Flores, Ph.D.,

Angel Jannasch-Pennell, Ph.D.,

Ruth Reynoso, M.Ed.

www.KOI-Education.com

PBS Tier 1 Manual, 4th Edition, International Edition 1.4

© 2012–2021 KOI Education

All rights reserved. No part of this publication may be reproduced, distributed, or transmitted in any form or by any means, including photocopying, recording, or other electronic or mechanical methods, without the prior written permission of the publisher, except in the case of brief quotations embodied in critical reviews and certain other noncommercial uses permitted by copyright law.

For permission requests, contact the publisher, info@koi-education.com,
Subject: "Written Permission Request".

All education documents, PBS templates and resources available from KOI-Education.com website are licensed under a Creative Commons Attribution-NonCommercial-ShareAlike 3.0 Unported License.

IISBN-13: 978-0-9982501-1-3 (eBook)
ISBN-13: 978-0-9982501-2-0 (Paperback)

Contents

Chapter 1 Introduction 5

Chapter 2 Teams 23

Chapter 3 Ownership System 35

Chapter 4 Assessment System 47

Chapter 5 Expectation System 63

Chapter 6 Teaching System 73

Chapter 7 Reinforcement System 83

Chapter 8 Accountability System 97

Chapter 9 Teaching Accountability 113

Chapter 10 Data Analysis 121

Chapter 11 Roll Out System 135

Chapter 12 Maintenance System 147

Chapter 13 Acknowledgements 159

Forward

"Positive Behaviour Support creates a more effective learning environment by making schools more predictable, consistent, positive and safe.."

—Dr. Robert Horner

The international edition of the PBS Manuals provides school teams with the guiding principles, evidence-based practices, templates, and step-by-step process required to create a high fidelity Positive Behavior Support (PBS) system the first time. All the elements are here to implement a PBS and Multi-Tiered framework that is culturally responsive for your staff, students, and community. Within a year, schools can measurably improve student learning and well-being while decreasing problem behaviours.

This interactive eBook includes photo galleries, embedded videos, full-page templates, and examples from schools implementing PBS around the globe.

Inside

- Expectation matrix tips and trips, plus four essential elements of a PBS poster

- Four part reinforcement system, it's not just tickets

- Three things adults must say before giving students a ticket in order for it to be effective

- Pros/Cons of school stores vs raffle vs digital reinforcement

- Why a four part accountability (consequence) system is critical to avoid dirty data

- How to organise a high profile PBS Kick Off and Roll Out's to four stakeholder groups

- Strategies to maintain, sustain and evaluate PBS to ensure outcomes

- Action plans and free resources are provided at the end of each chapter

What education leaders are saying about KOI PBS Manuals...

"I think you have seamlessly drawn together the very best of the best in behaviour research and implementation science to create this high quality PBS Manual. You walk the talk and model your beliefs throughout - I think you have achieved the gold standard."
—Jane Bennett, PBL District Coordinator, Catholic Education Melbourne, Melbourne, Australia

"The KOI PBS Tier 1, 2 and 3 Manuals are a fantastic resource and support for any school in building a high reliability and high fidelity PBS system. Practical, easy to use and well supported with resources."
—Brad Moyle, Principal, Wangaratta High School, Wangaratta, Australia

"Our schools positive climate change is directly attributed to the KOI Education training and manuals.?
—Trevor Herny, Principal, St.Paul's College, Melbourne, Australia

"As a teacher, I found it quick and easy to implement PBS using the activities and Action Plans in this manual. My school team was able to skip the trial and error process and implement a complete system that worked immediately in our school - which all staff and families loved!?
—Ruth Cornell, School-Wide Positive Behaviour Support Coach, Department of Education and Training, Victoria, Australia

THIS PAGE INTENTIONALLY LEFT BLANK

Chapter 1
Introduction

"IF THERE IS ANYTHING WE WISH TO CHANGE IN THE CHILD, WE SHOULD FIRST EXAMINE IT AND SEE WHETHER IT IS NOT SOMETHING THAT COULD BETTER BE CHANGES IN OURSELVES."

—CARL JUNG

Introduction

Learning Objectives

Identify the Elements, Principles and Outcomes of PBS

Examine Tier 1 Practices

Review Video Testimonials

 **Movie 1.1 Introduction to PBS**

Dr. Gulchak and Dr. Flores compare PBS to Cajun Cooking, you will always remember the main elements of PBS after watching! View at http://youtu.be/9BRRJQkVneU

 Movie 1.2 Creating the Culture of PBS

Produced for the National Center on Positive Behavioural Interventions and Supports. http://vimeo.com/3744737

Preview

What is Positive Behaviour Supports?

There are many parts and pieces to PBS that you may have heard about or experienced yourself. You may already know that PBS is a multi-tiered system - not a packaged program. It is often described as a framework that can be used and adapted to fit the culture and climate of a school. Teachers and staff have the opportunity to create their own school-wide expectations, teach these expectations, reinforce students when they meet the expectations and hold students accountable for misbehaviour. Therefore, PBS offers an opportunity to create an environment that is predictable, consistent, equitable and safe for all stakeholders.

PBS is not new or a "fad". The National Technical Assistance Center for PBS has been supported by the US Department of Education for over 20 years.

PBS is research based, evidence-based, practiced in across the globe and is installed by several countries all around the world. PBS is rooted in the science of Positive Behaviour Supports and prevention research which has been proven effective for all types of students since the early 1980s.

At its heart, PBS is about building strong relationships and supporting the whole child. The multi-tiered framework supports ALL students with the goal of meeting everyone's academic, social, emotional, and behavioural success.

Watch the video, *Creating the Culture of PBS*, to see PBS in action and hear from teachers, principals and parents from elementary through high school.

As you watch, consider the following questions:

- What ideas resonate with you?
- What ideas are familiar based on prior knowledge or experiences in schools?
- What are some new ideas and thoughts to share with others?

Identify the Elements, Principles and Outcomes of PBS

PBS is often referred to as a Multi-Tiered System of Supports (MTSS). Consider this analogy for understanding the application of a multi-tiered system of support:

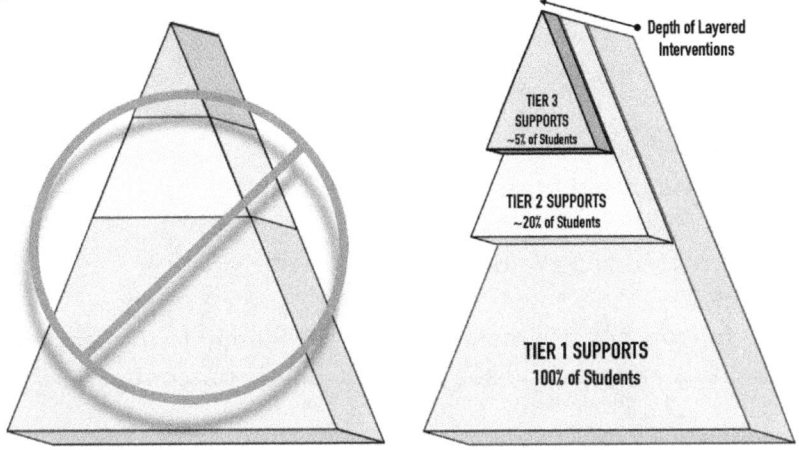

C.Guinn (2019), adapted from Education and Community Supports, University of Oregon.

Catching a cold or flu can often run rampant through a school campus. But there is a simple solution that, if everyone in the school implemented consistently, would cut down 80-90% of colds and flu. Wash hands! Washing hands with soap is a universal or Tier 1 intervention that can be implemented school-wide for all students and staff that would drastically reduce getting infected with a cold or flu.

But, some students and staff may still get sick. For this small group, interventions are often cough and cold medicine, cough candies, or the occasional over-the-counter pain and fever reducers. This is called a targeted or Tier 2 intervention. Should these staff and students stop washing their hands while taking cough medicine? Absolutely not! They continue with Tier 1 universal supports while also receiving the additional targeted supports.

However, even with Tier 1 and Tier 2 supports, a few of these students and staff may become even sicker. They may need to go to their doctor or the hospital to treat a severe case of influenza, pneumonia, or another more serious infection. This is treated on a case-by-case basis and is considered individualised or Tier 3 interventions. However, even though these students and staff are receiving secondary and tertiary support, they still need to implement universal precautions of washing their hands.

Treating the cold or flu requires a continuum of support. In school, PBS, because it is a multi-tiered system, provides a continuum of support. All students receive universal interventions, some students receive targeted interventions and a few students will need individualised interventions. When there are strong primary (Tier 1) interventions in place and PBS is implemented with integrity and fidelity, fewer and fewer students will need secondary (Tier 2) and tertiary (Tier 3) behavioural supports.

PBS Elements

According to the National Technical Assistance Center on Positive Behavioral Supports, PBS emphasises four integrated elements:

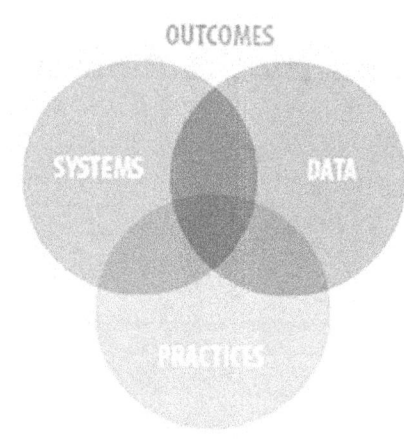

1. **Systems** that efficiently and effectively support the implementation of these practices
2. **Data** for decision making
3. **Practices** with evidence that these outcomes are achievable
4. **Outcomes** supported and evaluated by data

This book will show schools how to implement all PBS Elements to meet high implementation fidelity standards and see the measurable outcome.

PBS Principles

Six important principles are at the heart of PBS. The purpose of this manual is to teach school teams to implement these principles through an evidence-based and step-by-step process.

- Offer a continuum of scientifically-based behaviour interventions for students
- Arrange the learning environment to prevent the development and occurrence of problem behaviours
- Always monitor student performance
- Use data to make decisions and solve problems
- Teach and encourage prosocial behaviour skills
- Evaluate our implementation for integrity/fidelity

PBS Outcomes

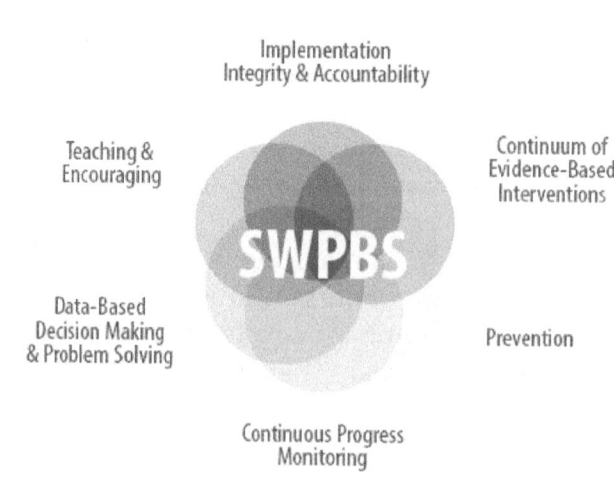

Schools that implement PBS with integrity and accountability can expect measurable changes in school culture, climate and safety. Positive outcomes have been repeatedly and empirically demonstrated for over 20 years in elementary through high school environments, for general and special education students, in urban and rural areas, as well as in early childhood, juvenile correction and home environments. See Gallery 1.1 for examples. Some proven outcomes include:

Proven PBS Outcomes	
✔ Decrease problem behaviour	✔ Improve organisational efficiency
✔ Increase academic performance	✔ Reduce staff turnover
✔ Increase attendance	✔ Equitable and positive environments
✔ Improve perception of safety	✔ Improve social emotional competence
✔ Reduce bullying behaviours	

With PBS, schools will be able to track behaviour problems on campus on a moment-by-moment basis in order to solve problems quickly and focus more time on academic instruction, relationships and student success. See Gallery 1.2.

Data entered into PBISapps.org since 2000 highlight that over 25,000 schools in the United States have implemented School-wide PBS (2018). More than 9,500 schools met high fidelity evaluation standards for Tier 1 implementation. Over 3,900 schools met Tier 2 fidelity criterion and more than 2,100 met Tier 3 fidelity measures. See Gallery 1.3.

PBS is also implemented in a growing list of countries worldwide. Visit the Association for Positive Behavior Support website (APBS.org) to connect with a global network of PBS researchers, educators and implementors. Join the Association to be a part of the movement and stay current with the latest PBS research, professional development, webinars and events.

 Gallery 1.1 Real Outcomes in Real Schools

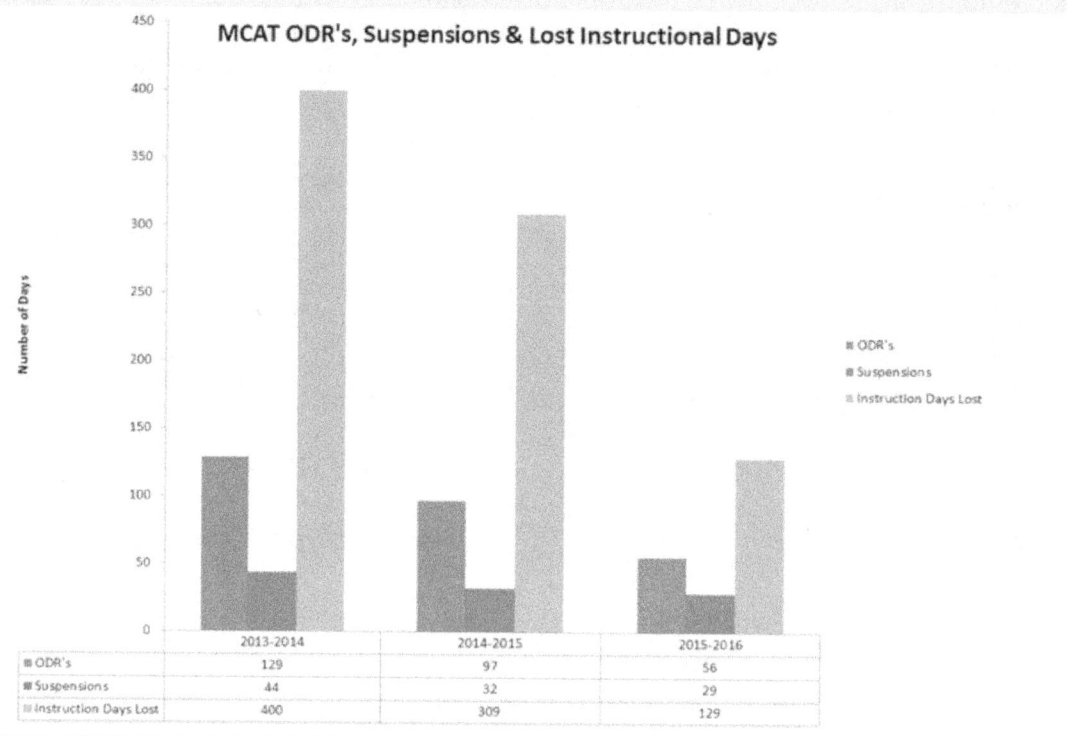

	2013-2014	2014-2015	2015-2016
ODR's	129	97	56
Suspensions	44	32	29
Instruction Days Lost	400	309	129

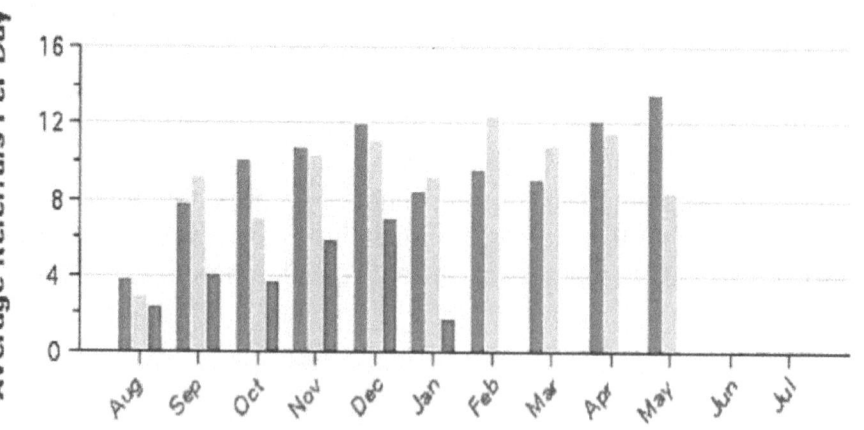

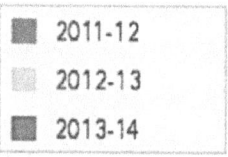

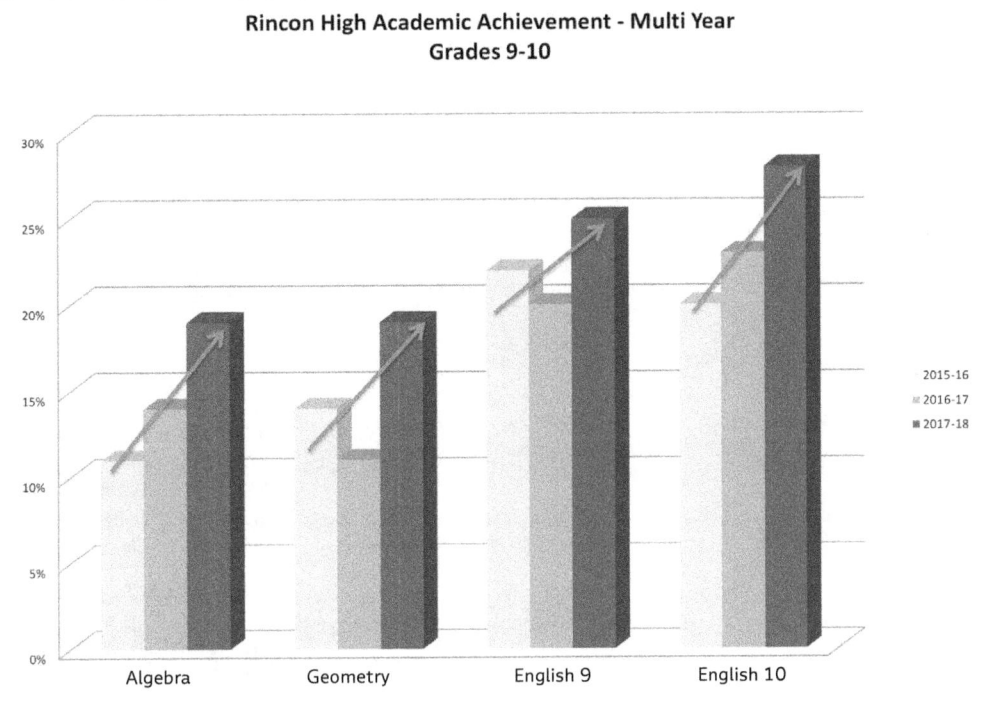

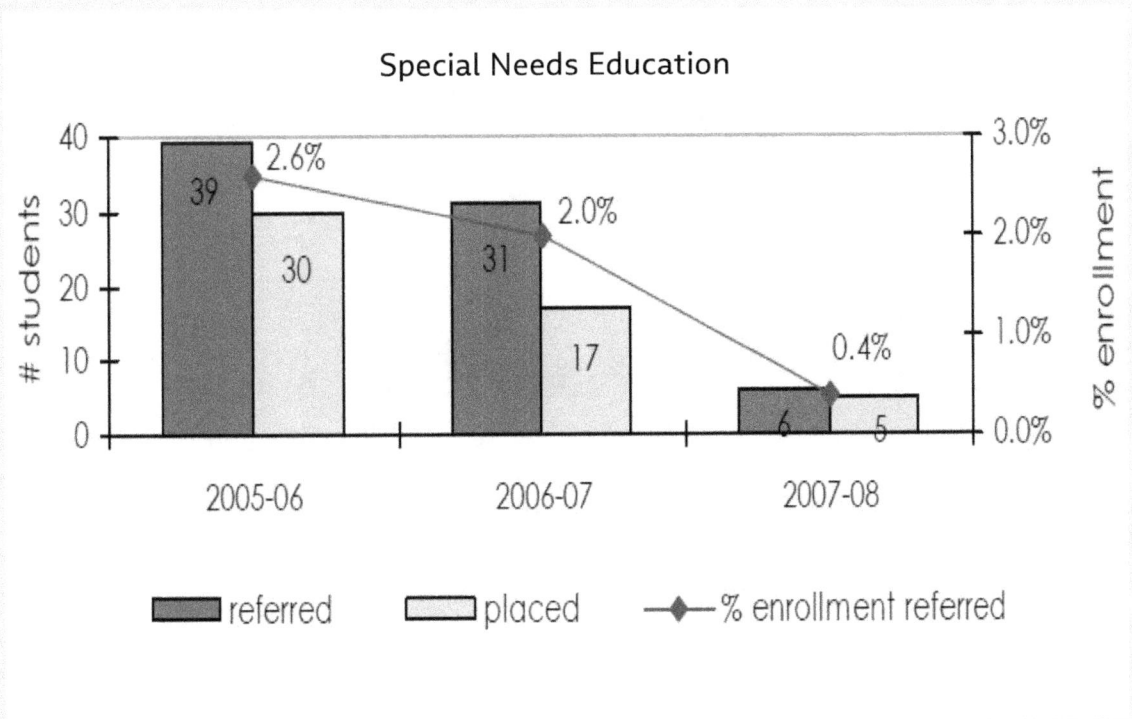

Gallery 1.2 Data, Data, Data!
Data dashboard from SWIS database, available from PBISapps.org (part of the National Technical Assistance Center for PBIS)

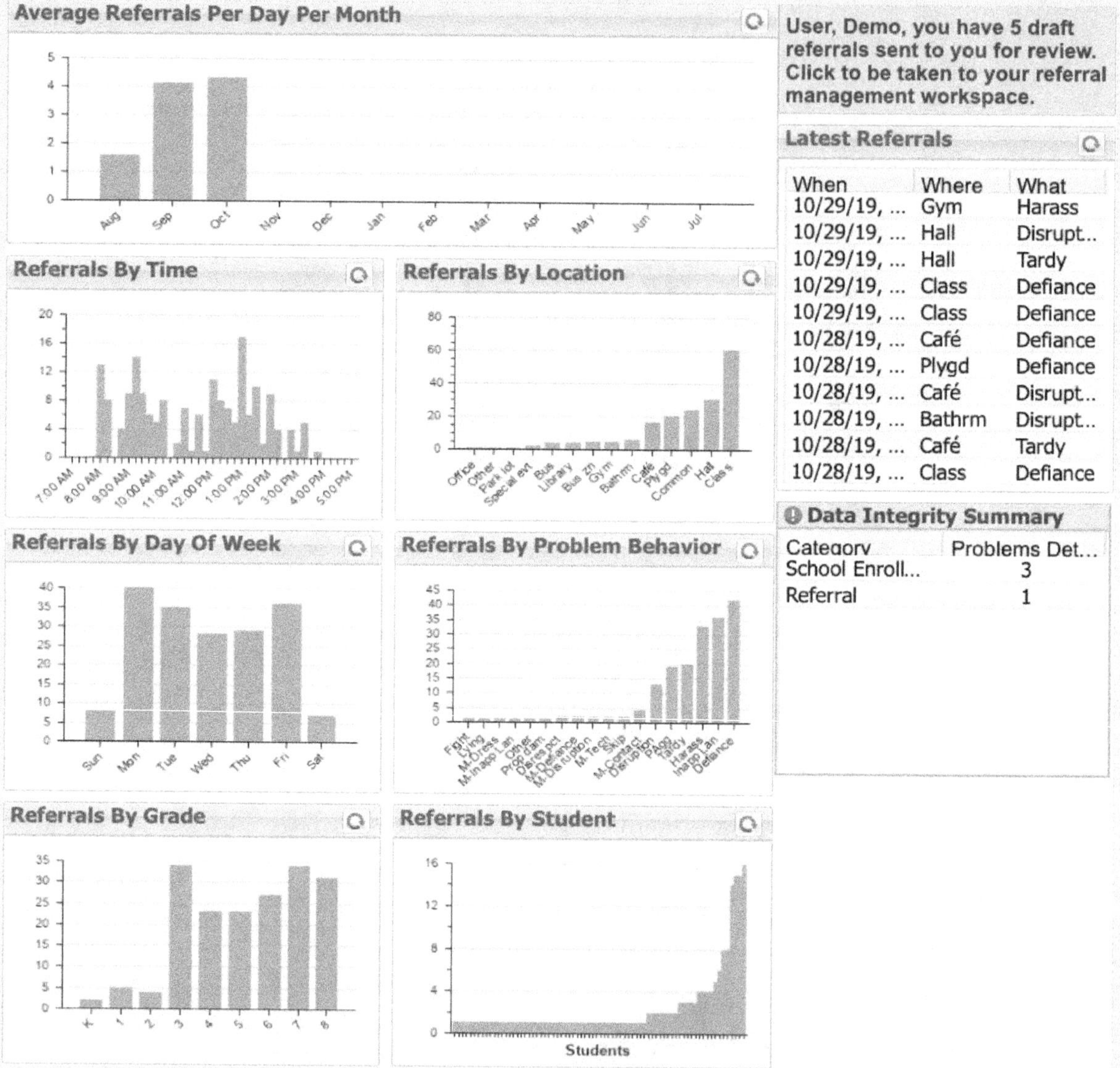

Gallery 1.3 Growth of PBS
Data from PBISapps.org

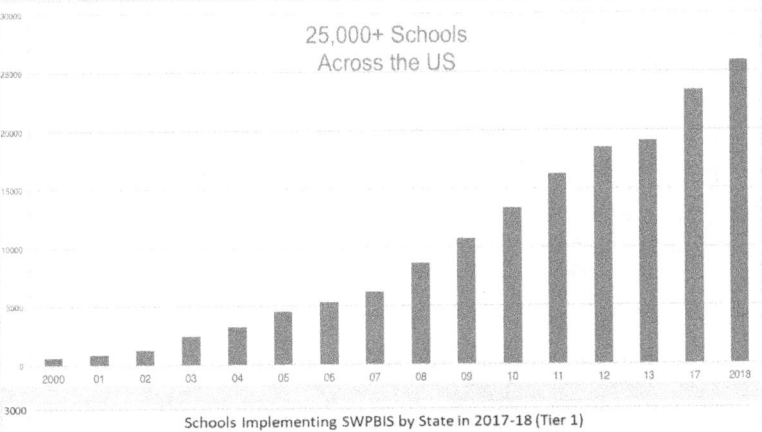

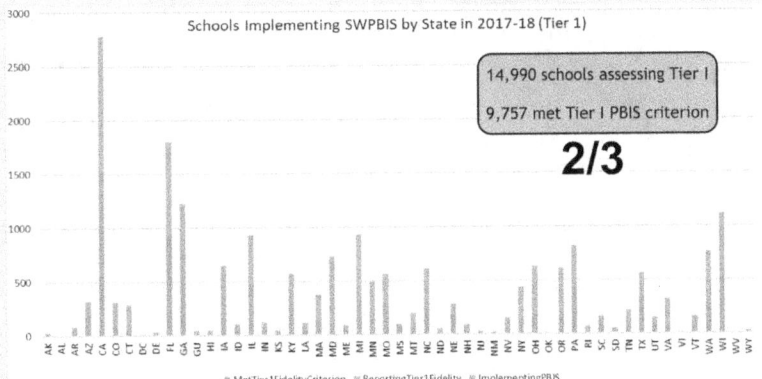

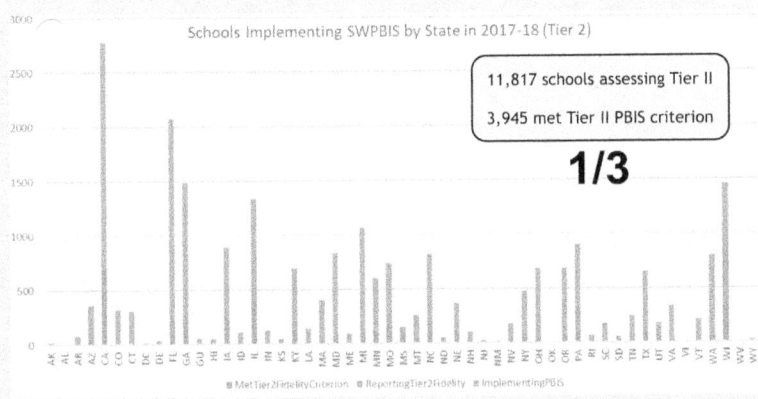

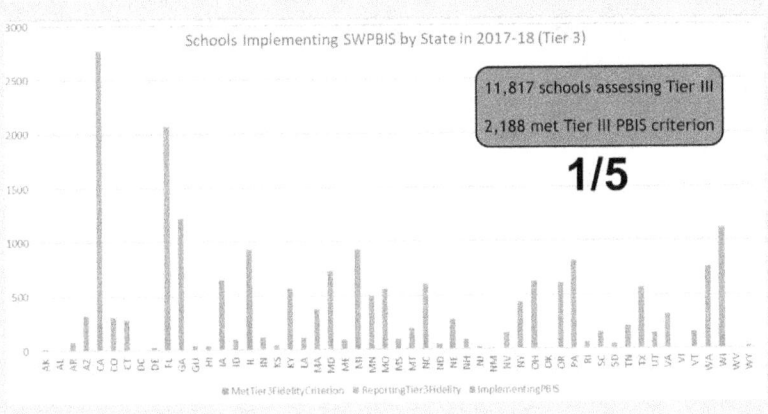

Examine Tier 1 Practices

As noted earlier, PBS provides a multi-tiered system of supports to students experiencing problem behaviours. These supports exist along a continuum - students should not be referred to as a Tier 1, Tier 2 or Tier 3 student. But rather, a student may need Tier 1 supports for getting along with peers in class, Tier 2 supports for reading, and maybe Tier 3 supports for anxiety on the playground or as an athlete on the high school football team. This book focuses on helping school teams implement Tier 1 PBS systems, data and practices for all students. Let's examine the four core practices that staff will implement in schools on a regular basis.

Creating Expectations

PBS is not a rigid program. It is a framework for providing preventative support. Schools get to choose the Expectations (values, traits, characteristic) that reflect the culture they want to promote.

The most common Expectations are Be Respectful, Be Responsible and Be Safe but many schools choose other Expectations as well. Expectations should be posted in common locations around the school to remind students (and staff) of the values that are expected to be practiced at school. See Gallery for a few examples.

For more details see the Expectation Systems Chapter.

Gallery 1.4 Expectation Examples

Cerbat Elementary School

Desiderata Alternative High School

Nautilus and Loma Linda Elementary Schools

Tonopah High School

Teaching Expectations

Complete the following statements:

- If students can't read, we _____
- If students can't write, we _____
- If students can't play the piano, we _____
- If students can't behave, we _____

We bet that people quickly and easily said, "Teach" for the first three statements, but may have paused for the last one. Why? Too often we treat behaviour skills different from academic or other life skills. But like academics and playing the piano, behaviour skills must be taught before we can (or before we should) expect students to master those skills. We should not assume that students know how to behave in school before being taught the necessary skills any more than we should assume a student knows calculus or chemistry before they have been taught.

Since every person in school is likely to have a different perception and personal definition of Expectations based on their prior experience and even based on their culture, it will be important to spend time as a staff to define and agree to common skills or rules that define each Expectation in different locations around the school. Respect may look like "Keep hands and feet to yourself" in the classroom or learning areas, but mean "Say please and thank you" in the cafeteria or lunchroom. See Gallery for posters with different expectations and skills.

For more details see the Teaching System Chapter.

Gallery 1.5 Expectation Posters

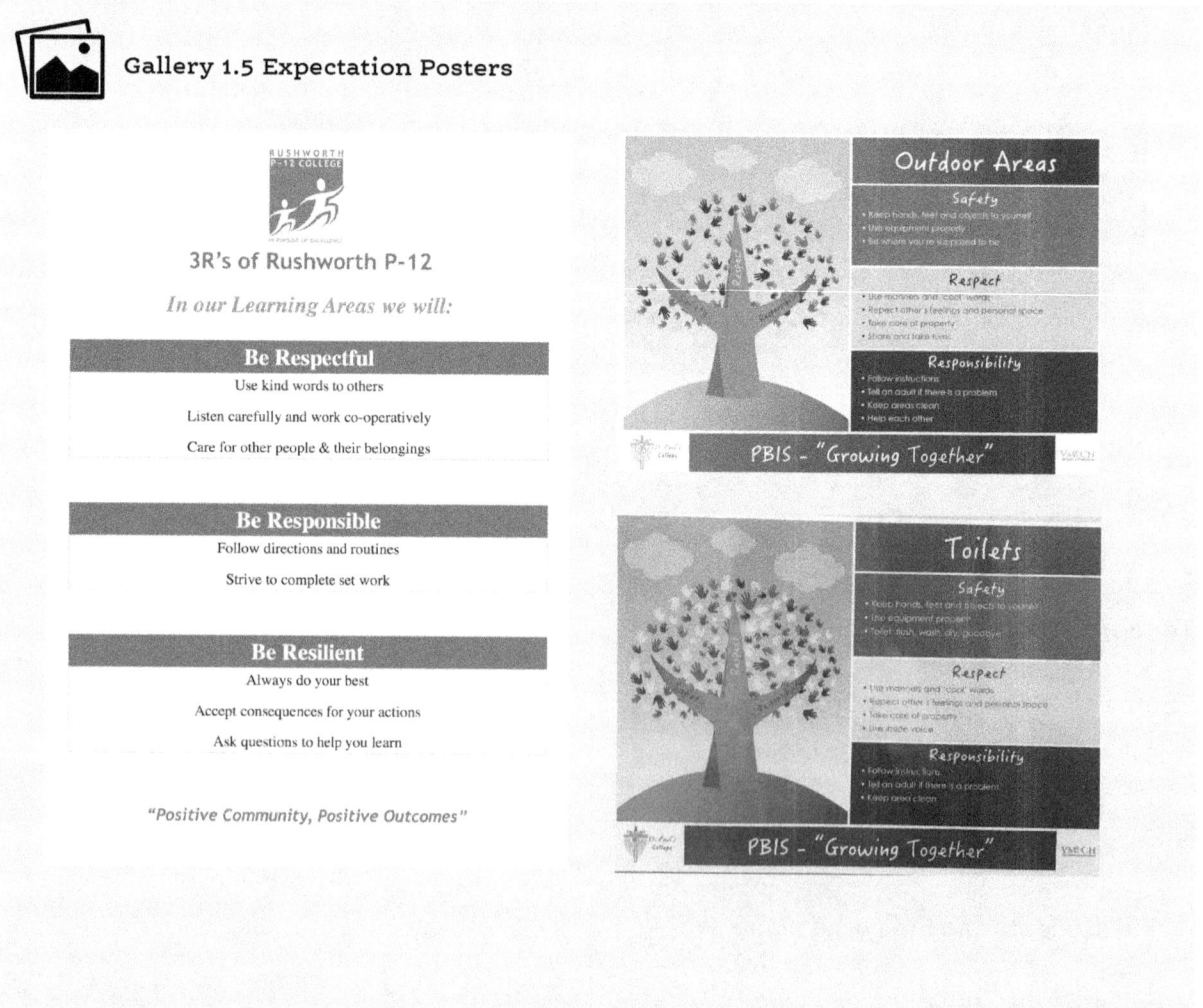

Reinforcing Expectations

In academics, we acknowledge and reinforce students for learning and demonstrating the correct skills and answers in their academic work. We give high fives, stickers, grades and more. Why can't we do the same for meeting our behavioural Expectations and skills?

One example of a reinforcement system comes from Payson Elementary School. Let's say a student returns his homework and a teacher reinforces him with a ticket and says, "Thanks for being responsible and returning your homework, Johnny", as this is an Expectation and Skill at the school. This is the first reinforcement. Johnny then takes the ticket to turn in to the school secretary who asks, " Why did you receive a ticket?". Johnny tells her that he received it for being Responsible and returning his homework, to which she replies, "Great work! I'm proud of you for being Responsible", and then puts his name on a Paw and displays it on the Panther Hall of Fame wall. This is the second reinforcement for returning his homework.

Later in the week Johnny's class is walking by the wall and Johnny tells his friends, "That's my ticket, and so is this one and that other one!" to a chorus of, "Way to go!" from his buddies. Reinforcement number 3.

At the end of the month, Johnny's grandmother is in school for a concert and he proudly shows her all the tickets he has received for being Responsible in school. His grandmother gives him a big hug and shares how much she loves him for working so hard in school. This is the fourth reinforcement for bringing his homework to school one-time. What are the chances that Johnny will bring his homework in next week?

For more details see the Reinforcement System Chapter.

Accountability to the Expectations

Is discipline at your school:

- Consistent across all staff?
- Predictable across all staff?
- Equitable across all staff?

Can you answer "Yes" to these questions about accountability for behaviour at your school? If not, what does this tell us?

Now try these questions:

- Do all staff know what behaviours should be handled in the classroom or which should be sent to the office?
- Are there staff who never write referrals for a behaviour problem because they handle everything in the classroom on their own?
- Are there staff who write too many referrals, for any perceived behaviours?
- Are consequences and student discipline handled the same way by all administrators?

If the answer is "No" to any question, then there is not a consistent, predictable or equitable system for holding students accountable to school-wide expectations. This can be very confusing for students as well as staff.

A solution to all these problems is a Behaviour Flowchart. A flowchart provides consistency to accountability systems.

Behaviour Flowchart

- ✔ Identifies classroom managed vs office managed behaviour problems
- ✔ Lists procedures for interviewing consistently in the classroom or other areas of the school for minor problems
- ✔ Specifies when to report a minor behaviour to the office
- ✔ Lists procedures for administrators when deciding on consequences
- ✔ Keeps staff and students on the same page

For more details see the Accountability System Chapter, Teaching Accountability Chapter and Data Analysis Chapter.

Behaviour Flowchart

Rushworth P12 College

Observe Student Behavior

Managed by STAFF	MINOR Behaviour	MAJOR Behaviour	Managed by TEAM LEADERS
Intervention 1 **Remind**: Provide a verbal or visual reminder of 3R's at Rushworth. **Intervention 2** **Reteach**: Reteach the 3R that is not being followed, document on Minor Behaviour Tracking Form. **Intervention 3: Parent Contact** **Remove +/or Reflect**: Relocate student within the classroom and assign a Reflection Activity or Loss of Privilege. Contact parent and document on Minor Behaviour Tracking Form. **Intervention 4** **Report**: Complete an ODR Form, attach Minor Behaviour Tracking Form and turn in to Team Leaders.	Disrespect (talking back) Defiance (work refusal) Disruption (yelling/interrupting) Uniform Profanity Electronic Device (phone, etc.) Lying, Cheating, Forgery Homework Leaving class Stealing (petty theft) Non-Compliance	Physical Aggression Verbal Aggression Threats Stealing (major theft) Vandalism/Graffiti Drugs/Alcohol Weapons Harassment Bullying Racism	**Step 1: Parent Contact** Complete an ODR Form and conference with student to review 3R's at Rushworth. **Step 2** Assign consequence according to school policies. **Step 3** Provide feedback to staff on ODR outcome. Document to SWIS. **Step 4** Complete ODR data entry. Document to SWIS.

Classroom Management

Interventions start over at the beginning of each week.

Use prevention strategies such as teaching/practicing expectations, teaching routines, 1:4 ratio of positive to negative feedback, physical layout of class, increase academic engagement, increase academic success, increase opportunities to respond, vary modes of Instruction, etc. Please remember to Use strategies detailed in Classroom Instruction That Works and Teach Like a Champion: both are available in the College Library

2015_Flowchart_RushworthP12

Positive Community - Positive Outcomes

Review Video Testimonials

It is getting easier to find testimonials from educators about using a PBS System in their schools. Check out these comments from experienced colleagues.

> ## Reflection
>
> *What are the common themes and ideas that educators say they value in their PBS systems?*

Movie 1.3 Shawn Goodwin, Elementary School Principal
Nautilus Elementary, Lake Havasu USD http://youtu.be/Bnf9KB3s7qk

Movie 1.4 Lori Mora, Middle School Assistant Principal
Deer Valley Middle School, Deer Valley USD http://youtu.be/Ol7kd94nFng

Movie 1.5 Grace Kopp, High School Counsellor
Creating the Culture of PBIS https://vimeo.com/3744737

With this PBS Tier 1 Manual schools will be able to implement all the elements and principles of PBS with integrity, fidelity and outcomes!

Figure 1.1 PBS Tier 1 Graphic Organiser

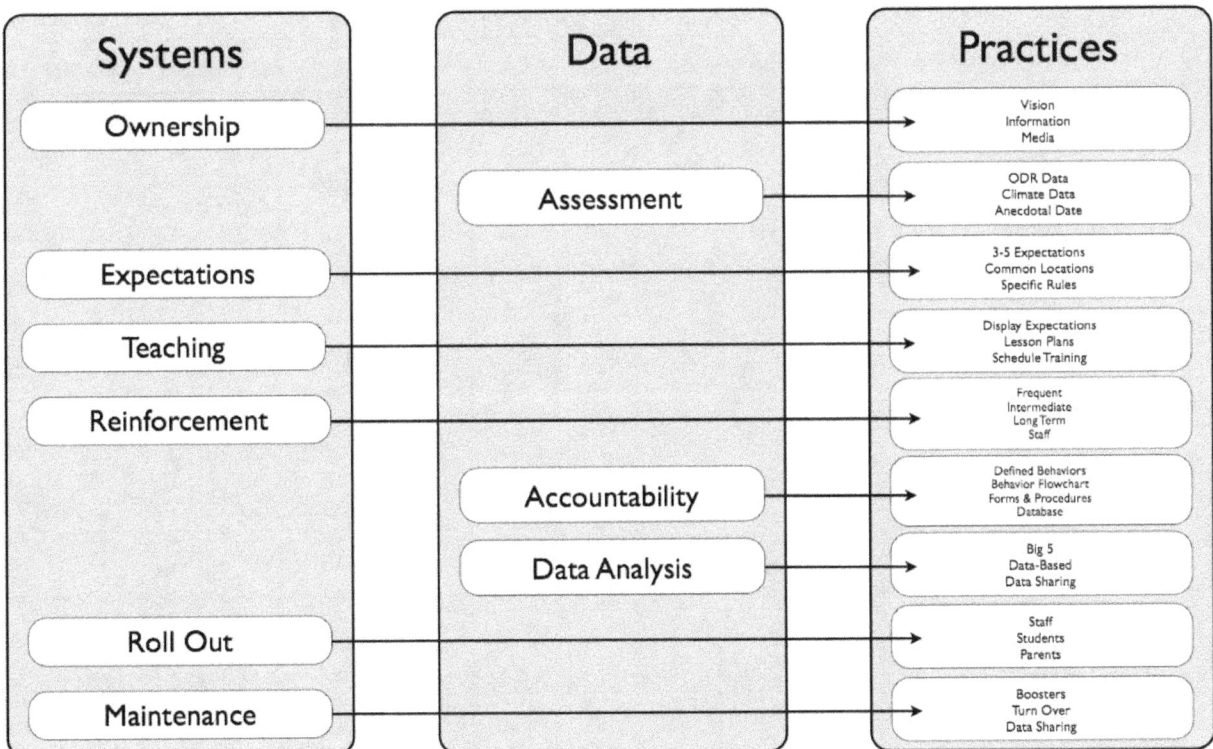

THIS PAGE INTENTIONALLY LEFT BLANK

Chapter 2
Teams

"SO MANY OF OUR DREAMS AT FIRST SEEM IMPOSSIBLE, THEN THEY SEEM IMPROBABLE, AND THEN, WHEN WE SUMMON THE WILL, THEY SOON BECOME INEVITABLE."

—CHRISTOPHER REEVE (ACTOR, SUPERMAN)

Teams

Learning Objectives

Identify District Team Goals

Identify School Team Goals

Select Member Roles & Assign Responsibilities

Explore Team Documentation

Many of us have had the pleasure of being on numerous committees throughout our career. Some of those experiences may have been productive, others not so much.

But, how many teams have you been a part of and what is the difference between a team and a committee? Why does PBS and systems change take a team?

When we say TEAM, think of:
- A football team that works together to get a ball across the goal line.
- A baseball team that works together to bring in runs.
- A basketball team that works together to get a ball through a hoop.

Teams work together toward a common predetermined goal—that is also what is needed for a systems change, like PBS.

Preview

Systems change cannot be successful with only one individual leading the change—it takes a team. One issue in some schools is that we interchange the term 'team' with 'committee'. Committees are made up of people with various purposes, goals, and agendas. A team works together toward a common predetermined goal.

Team Characteristics

A differentiating factor between teams and committees is the fact that teams work together for a common, specified end goal. They need to have a:
- Common purpose
- Common goal
- Common agenda

PBS Systems Require Two Teams

District and school teams each have different roles, goals and responsibilities:

A **District Team** provides guidance, support and resources to a school team.

A **School Team** creates and implements school-wide, targeted, and individual interventions to help students succeed.

Identify District Team Goals

Over 20 years of research and real-world implementation supports the notion that PBIS sustainability at the school-level requires the support of the district and state-level leadership teams. Fortunately, the National Technical Assistance Centre on Positive Behavioural Interventions and Supports has a detailed action planning document for teams. What used to be known as the PBIS Implementation and Planning Self-Assessment (AKA - PBIS Blueprint) has evolved into the District System Fidelity Inventory (DSFI).

The purpose of the District Systems Fidelity Inventory (DSFI) is to guide District Leadership Teams in the assessment, development, and execution of action plans that promote the capacity for sustainable, culturally and contextually relevant, and high-fidelity implementation of multi-tiered social, emotional, and behavioural systems of support and practices.
– Technical Assistance Centre on Positive Behavioural Interventions and Supports (2021)

Further Reading

George, H. P., & Kincaid, D. K. (2008). Building district-level capacity for positive behaviour support. Journal of Positive Behaviour Interventions, 10, 20–32.

George, H. P., Cox, K. E., Minch, D. & Sandomiersk, T. (2018). District practices associated with successful SWPBIS implementation. Behavioural Disorders, 43, 393– 406.

District Team Goals

The DSFI identifies the following nine categories as critical to building, maintaining, and sustaining PBIS systems across multiple school settings.

1. Leadership Teaming
2. Stakeholder Engagement
3. Funding and Alignment
4. Policy
5. Workforce Capacity
6. Training
7. Coaching
8. Evaluation
9. Local Implementation Demonstrations

Each category is defined by several features or objectives, data sources for each feature, and a scoring criteria rubric for leadership teams to use when evaluating their progress. The DSFI items can be added to an action plan that guides implementation over 3-5 years and updated a few times per year to assess progress.

Diagram 2.1 District Team Goals
Download from koi-education.com/resources

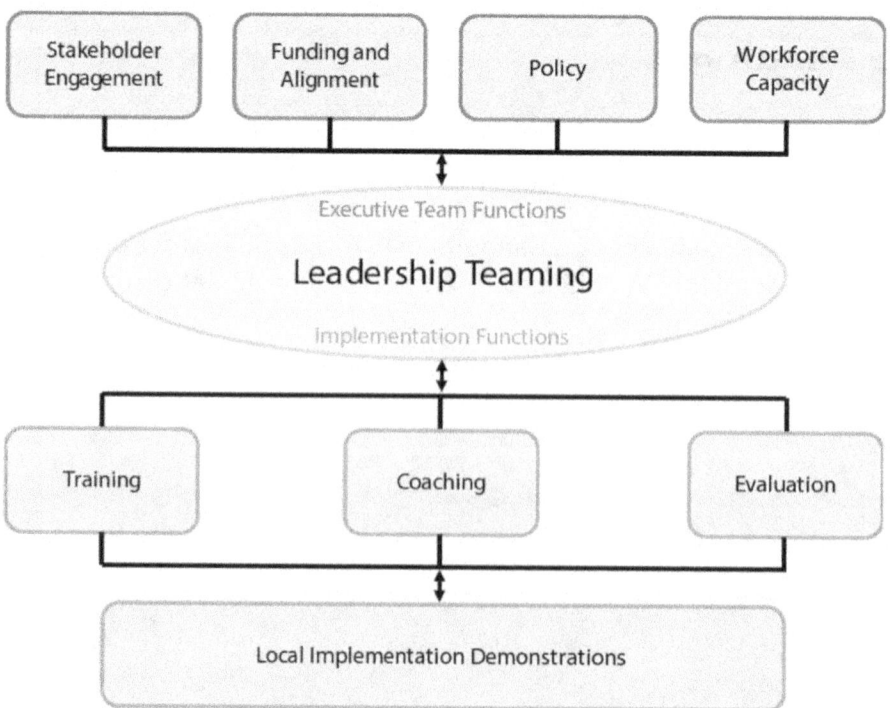

District Team Members

The DSFI specifies that the District Leadership Team should be facilitated by a coordinator(s) with designated time for coordination and with experience in data-based decision-making. It must include one or more leaders with the authority to make key decisions such as district/school budgets, implementation mandates, policy decisions, and authorizing data systems adoption or changes. Team members should also include individuals representing Preschools through grade 12 and with social-emotional-behavioural expertise across the full continuum of behaviour support (Tiers 1, 2, 3). A broad group of stakeholders should represent the following departments or offices:

- Superintendent
- General education
- Special education
- Professional development
- Information technology
- Transportation
- Assessment/Evaluation
- School psychology, counselling, and social work
- Social-emotional-behavioural experts
- School Principals
- School Board
- Family/community

Identify School Team Goals

School Teams are the core for creating and sustaining systems change initiatives, but they cannot operate in a vacuum. Teams must make every effort to solicit and provide feedback to the school community as often as possible. The fidelity of your system depends on it.

School Team Goals

Here are some of the major goals of a school PBS team in the first year of planning:
- Build buy-in, ownership, and communication with all stakeholders
- Assess school climate, fidelity, and student progress
- Create, teach, and reinforce expectations
- Develop an accountability and data-analysis system
- Plan for initial rollout and sustainability

As a prerequisite for beginning PBS, schools should complete a School Readiness Agreement similar to the one identified at PBISaz.org. This document is similar or identical to those created by other statewide PBS organisations and is based on the Implementation Blueprint framework.

School Team Members

According to PBS research, members of the **Tier 1 PBS school team** must include a diverse group of stakeholders including:
1. Principal
2. General Education Teacher
3. Special Education Teacher
4. Non-Classroom Staff (paraprofessional, related services, security, etc.)
5. School Psychologist or Behaviour Specialist
6. Parent
7. Student (optional for K-8, required for high school)

Tier 2 and Tier 3 PBS school teams are composed of individuals with more specialised knowledge regarding behaviour interventions. These individuals may include: special education teachers, school psychologist, counsellor, social worker, behaviour interventionist or Board Certified Behaviour Analyst, and mental health professional.

If team members do not take roles and responsibilities seriously, then they will end up doing what they have always done – that is, work as a committee.

- Carol Scearce (School Teams Expert)

Select Team Member Roles & Assign Responsibilities

Teams work best when everyone has a defined role and responsibility. In baseball, for example, there are pitchers, catchers, and fielders. In schools, we have administrators, teachers and support staff. Each player has a responsibility. All teams function best when everyone performs their role.

Leader
Responsible for moving the team forward to accomplish goals by providing an Agenda and managing the team.

Facilitator
Responsible for the group process, team climate, and ensuring that everyone has a voice.

Recorder
Responsible for documenting team Minutes and recording decisions, strategies, person responsible and due dates on the team Action Plan.

Data Profiler
Responsible for collecting and analysing school data (ODRs, climate and fidelity surveys) to be shared with the team and all stakeholders.

Time Keeper
Responsible for keeping the team on task according to the Agenda so that time is used productively.

Team Member
Responsible for completing tasks between meetings and being a contributing participant.

Figure 2.1 Team Roles & Responsibilities
Download from koi-education.com/resources

Leader

The Team Leader is responsible for moving the team to accomplish its meeting tasks. The Leader should ensure an environment that helps the team get the work done. The Leader does not have to be the principal on your team.

Facilitator

The Team Facilitator makes things happen with ease.
The Team Facilitator helps the group with the process, with the "how" decisions, and with digging deeper for information.

Recorder

The Team Recorder is responsible for writing down the team's key points, ideas, process, and decisions recording only the facts and avoiding editorializing. Prior to each meeting the Recorder should review the agenda for action items. After each meeting the Recorder should send meeting minutes to all team members.

Data Profiler

The Data Profiler collects, organizes, and keeps the current data information relating to the needs of the project. The Data Profiler assists in interpreting and analyzing the data and shares data through graphs, displays, and reports to all stakeholders.

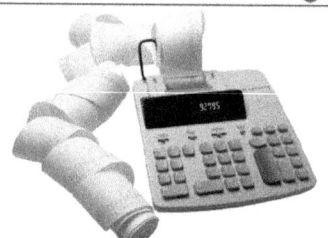

Time Keeper

The Timekeeper monitors how long the team is taking to accomplish its tasks and provides regular updates to the team on how well or how poorly they are using their time. If time becomes an issue the timekeeper will collaborate with the team to determine new time schedules and if the agenda needs to be adjusted.

Team Member

Team Members don't have specific responsibilities at the meeting, but fulfill duties between meetings; their participation is critical to the team's success. Team members must agree to: Be enthusiastic and committed to the team's purpose, Be honest and keep any confidential information behind closed doors, and Fulfill duties between meeting.

Team Roles and Responsibility adapted from www.didp.gov. Also search for *Tuckman's Stages of Group Development* for Forming, Storming, Norming, and Performing stages.

Explore Team Documentation

Documentation is essential for a system to be sustainable. The following team documents should be used regularly and maintained digitally as well as via hard copy in a team binder and/or cloud storage that is accessible to all team members and remains regularly available. All documents are available from koi-education.com/resources.

Team Charter
Record of team members, purpose, decision making process, norms, and meeting dates/times for the entire school calendar.

Team Roles & Responsibilities
Reminder of team roles and defined responsibilities at each meeting.

Team Agenda
Details the purpose of each meeting and the items needed to be discussed.

Team Minutes
A written record of meeting decisions including person responsible and timeline.

Action Plan
A table of desired outcomes, strategies, target date, resources needed, person responsible and status.

Working Smarter Matrix
A table that lists all the teams or committees at a school and details about their purpose. Use this matrix to identify overlap of initiatives or staff involvement. Consider merging or eliminating groups with similar goals so you can work smarter, not harder.

Interactive 2.1 Working Smarter Matrix

Download from koi-education.com/resources

Working Smarter Matrix

School Name: _____   School Year: _____

EXAMPLE

Initiative/ Committee	Purpose	Measureable Outcome	Target Group	Staff Involved	SIP/SID
Attendance Committee	Increase attendance	Increase % of students attending daily	All students	Eric, Ellen, Marlee	Goal #2
Character Education	Improve character	Weekly lessons	All students	Marlee, J.S., Ellen	Goal #3
Safety Committee	Improve safety	Safety response document	Dangerous students	Has not met	Goal #3
School Spirit Committee	Enhance school spirit	Assemblies	All students	Has not met	
Discipline Committee	Improve behavior	Decrease office referrals	Bullies, antisocial students, repeat offenders	Ellen, Eric, Marlee, Otis	Goal #3
DARE Committee	Prevent drug use	Decrease office referrals for drugs	High/at-risk drug users	Don	
PBIS Leadership Team	Implement 3-tier behavior system	Decrease office referrals and behavior problems, increase attendance, enhance academic engagement, improve grades	All students	Eric, Ellen, Marlee, Otis, Emma	Goal #2 Goal #3

Reflection

*Take a minute to reflect on PBS Teams.
How does the purpose of a District Team differ from a School Team?
Why are both necessary?*

Action Plan

1. Complete a Team Charter
2. Complete a Working Smarter Matrix
3. Download resources below (agenda, minutes, etc.)
4. Begin a PBS Team Folder/Binder (See Maintenance System Chapter for details and a suggested Table of Contents) to organise practices
5. Schedule/teach 'Behaviour Principles' book to staff
6. District Leadership Team invites stakeholders to review the District System Fidelity Inventory (DSFI) and create an Action Plan

Resources

- District System Fidelity Inventory (DSFI)
- Team Charter & Team Roles/Responsibilities
- Team Agenda & Team Minutes
- Working Smarter Matrix
- Team Binder/Folder - Table of Contents

Available from koi-education.com/resources

Evaluation

1. District goals include all of the following except:
   a. Policy
   b. Training capacity
   c. Behaviour capacity
   d. Marketing

2. School Teams must include parents:
   a. True
   b. False

3. Team roles include:
   a. Leader & Facilitator
   b. Recorder & Psychologist
   c. Data Profiler & Timer
   d. A and B
   e. A and C

4. A Team charter is optional:
   a. True
   b. False

Answers: 1d, 2a, 3e, 4b

Chapter 3
Ownership System

"LEARNING IS NOT ATTAINED BY CHANCE. IT MUST BE SOUGHT FOR WITH ARDOUR AND ATTENDED TO WITH DILIGENCE."

—ABIGAIL ADAMS (WIFE OF JOHN ADAMS, 2ND PRESIDENT OF USA)

Ownership System

Learning Objectives

Create a Team Vision

Share Information about PBS

Use Multiple Sources of Media

 Movie 3.1 Help Desk

Systems change takes time, planning, and determination. This parody video illustrates this point by looking at resisting change from using a scroll to using a textbook. Retrieved from http://youtu.be/OCd7Bsp3dDo

Preview

This introduction video is a great illustration that change takes time—systems change in schools must be treated the same way.

It will not happen by chance...and it will not come easy to some.

Three Parts of an Ownership System

The three parts of a school-wide PBS ownership system include the dissemination of:

- Vision
- Information
- Media

Gallery 3.1 Three Parts of the Ownership System

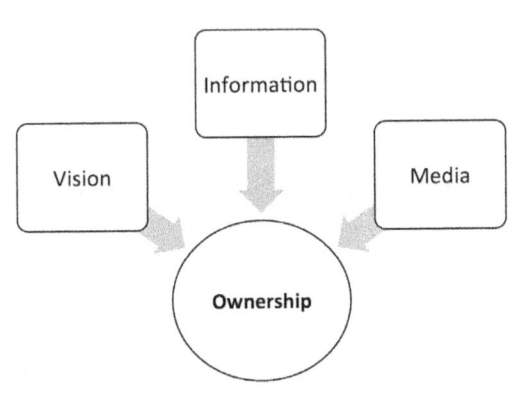
Ownership System Graphic

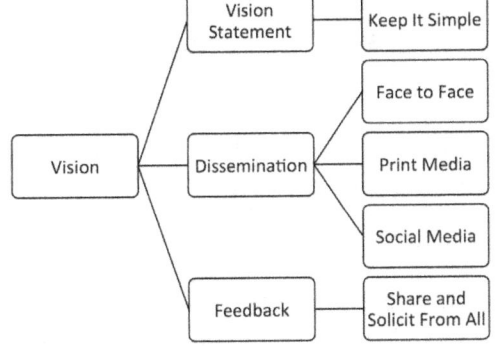
Vision

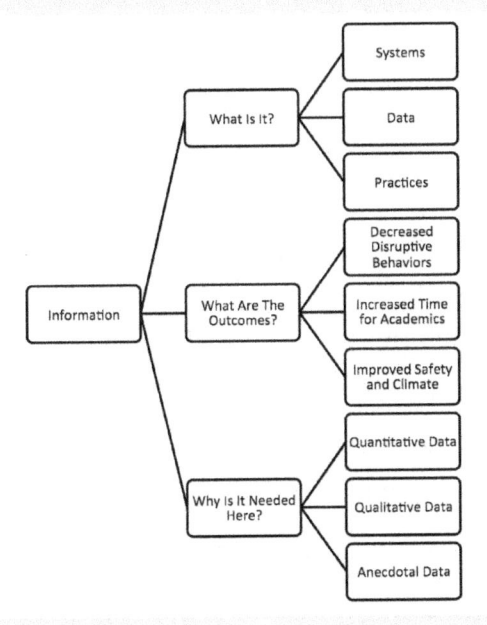
Information

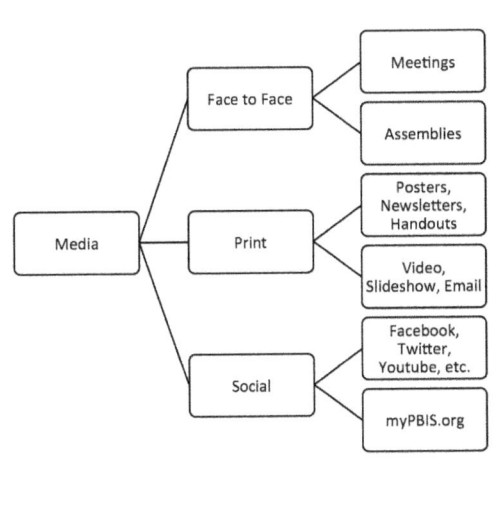
Media

Create a Team Vision

Change Can Come About in Two Ways

Top Down
An administrator or small group shouts change from the top down

Bottom Up:
A diverse team of stakeholders seeks input from and provides feedback to staff, students, and parents

Question?
- Which method takes longer?
- Which leads to high fidelity of implementation, long-term sustainability, and student outcomes?

The answer to both questions is: Bottom Up.

Vision Includes Three Parts

1) Vision
Spend time discussing your vision so that everyone in your school can move forward in the same direction. Keep it simple! Here are examples of organisational Visions:
- Phoenix Zoo: A world class zoo for a world class city.
- Starbucks: Inspire the human spirit - one person, one cup, and one neighbourhood at a time.
- Apple: Make a contribution to the world by making tools for the mind that advance humankind.
- PBS: Consistent and school-wide expectations and accountability for all.
- PBS: Support all students to succeed socially and academically every day.

2) Dissemination
Spend time sharing your Vision in multiple ways such as Face-to-Face, Print Media, and Social Media:
- Faculty meetings - regular or special agenda item
- Grade level or subject level team meetings - seek feedback ideas
- Posters/Bulletin Board/Paper Banners - change them frequently
- Newsletter/Newspaper/Email/Assembly - post draft documents
- Parent Teacher Associations/Organisations - share draft ideas and survey opinions

3) Feedback
Spend time asking and listening to questions and concerns. Then be sure to tell and show people that you heard them and considered their views.
- Climate survey data
- Office Discipline Referral data
- Online polls and surveys
- Post information in multiple formats
- Inform stakeholders about PBS Vision multiple times throughout the year

> *Vision*
> *People don't believe what you tell them.*
> *They rarely believe what you show them.*
> *They often believe what their friends tell them.*
> *They always believe what they tell themselves.*
>
> *Leaders give people stories they can tell themselves;*
> *stories about the future and about change.*
> — Seth Godin

See Gallery for examples of disseminating a PBS Vision.

Gallery 3.2 Vision & Dissemination
Got PBIS? Alhambra and South Mountain High Schools, Phoenix Union High School District.

Share Information About PBS

Before staff or students can buy-in to School-Wide PBS or vote for change, they need to know a little bit about the system and what's in it for them. Honestly, this is a never ending campaign. There will always be new staff or students to inform and people that want to cling to old ideas or paradigms.

A valuable resource is the **National Technical Assistance Center on Positive Behavioral Interventions and Support**, PBIS.org. At this site, you can find FAQs and information for schools, families, and the community including new research, evaluation tools, and training topics.

Three Information Elements Need To Be Shared To Increase Ownership

1) What Is PBS?
PBS is Systems, Data, and Practices that make school a more effective learning environment:
- PBS is a system and is not a program or curriculum
- PBS is school-wide, evidence-based, and used nationwide
- PBS catches students displaying proper behaviour and provides consistent consequences for disruptive behaviours
- PBS teaches and supports students so they can be socially and behaviourally successful
- PBS makes schools more predictable, consistent, positive, and safe for all staff and students

2) What Are PBS Outcomes?
- Decrease disruptive classroom behaviours and office referrals
- Increase time for academics and academic achievement
- Improve school climate and safety

3) Why Is PBS Needed Here?
Share Your Quantitative Data (Data Audit Tool)
- Share your current office discipline referrals, academic achievement scores, attendance rate, drop-out rate, failure rate, graduation rate, disproportionate suspension rates, and special education referral rates
- See the Assessment Systems Chapter in this manual for more details about using a Data Audit Tool

Share Your Qualitative Data (Climate Surveys)
- Share surveys from staff, student and parents showing their perceptions of the school climate and safety
- See the Assessment chapter in this manual for more details about using Climate Surveys

Share Your Anecdotal Data
- Share testimonials and success stories from research or teacher magazines, show videos from PBS schools, spotlight testimonials from staff or students who have been at PBS schools in other districts or states
- See and share the video testimonials on PBS at koi-education.com/success-stories

> *"Seek first to understand, then to be understood."*
> - Steven Covey, Author of 7 Habits of Highly Successful People

Use Multiple Sources of Media

Today, we are fortunate to have multiple methods to communicate and disseminate information. No one way is better than another. Always consider the audience when crafting your message and when you publish it.

Three Media Source Should Be Considered

1) Face To Face
Meetings and Assemblies

- Meetings, grade level, subject area, non-classroom, open houses, parent-teacher, etc.
- Student assemblies, special events, fairs, parties, sporting events, music and arts events, etc.

2) Print & Digital Media
- Posters, newsletter, flyers, and handouts can be sent directly to your target audience
- Email, video, and slide shows can be sent directly to your target audience

3) Social Media
- Facebook, Twitter, YouTube, Teacher Tube, Wikis, Blogs, etc.
- Custom myPBIS Website - myPBIS.org. See Gallery for myPBIS website examples.
- Use myPBIS as a digital interactive bulletin board for your school.
- Share: What is PBS, What are the outcomes, and Why is it needed here.
- Post Expectation posters, lesson plans, or videos.

Gallery 3.3 myPBIS.org

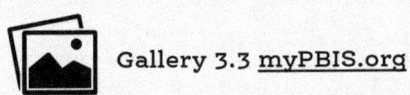

KOI Education will create a custom myPBIS PBS site for your school.

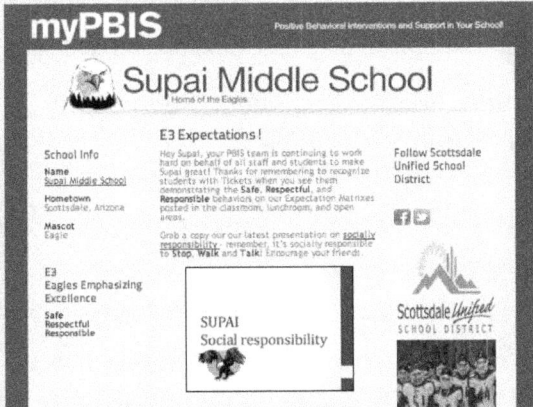
Supai Middle School, Scottsdale USD

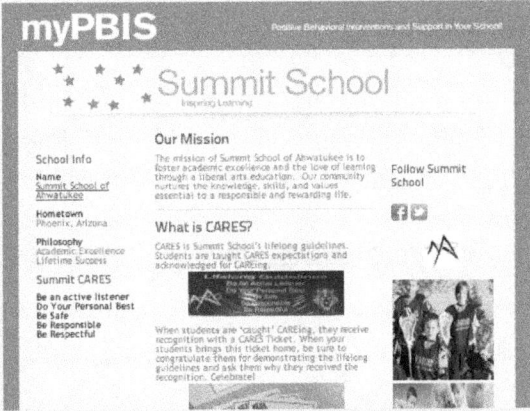
Summit School of Ahwatukee, Private School

Boulder Creek High School, Deer Valley USD

Paseo Hills Elementary School, Deer Valley USD

KOI Education can provide you with a customised and personalise myPBIS.org web domain for your PBS system and your PBS content. Visit the website to see an example.

Reflection

Take a minute to reflect on the importance of ownership and buy-in.
What are the three elements of an Ownership System?
Which will be most difficult for your PBS team to implement and why?

Action Plan

1. Create your team vision statement
2. Share information about PBS with staff, students and parents
3. Use multiple sources of media to share information
4. Submit content for your myPBIS.org custom website

Resources

- PBIS.org - see PBS FAQs, research and evaluation, PBS for Beginners, PBS in early childhood, classroom, high school, juvenile correction, etc.
- myPBIS.org, see example school web page

Available from koi-education.com/resources.

Evaluation

1. Change that leads to high fidelity of implementation, long-term sustainability, and student outcomes is:
   a. Impossible
   b. Bottom up
   c. A fuzzy dream
   d. Top down

2. Information that needs to be shared with all stakeholders beginning today includes:
   a. What is PBS
   b. What are the outcomes of PBS
   c. Why is PBS needed here
   d. All of the above

3. myPBIS is:
   a. A new TV sitcom
   b. A health insurance company for teachers
   c. A type of fungus found in New York City hot dog carts
   d. A digital interactive bulletin board for your school

Answers: 1b, 2d, 3d

THIS PAGE INTENTIONALLY LEFT BLANK

Chapter 4
Assessment System

"THE TEMPTATION TO FORM PREMATURE THEORIES UPON INSUFFICIENT DATA IS THE BANE OF OUR PROFESSION."

—SHERLOCK HOLMES

Assessment System

Learning Objectives

Use a Data Audit Tool (Quantitative)

Distribute Climate Surveys (Qualitative)

Collect Testimonial Data (Anecdotal)

Utilise PBISapps.org (Progress Monitoring)

The Age of Aquarius has long past - we now live in the Age of Accountability. But instead of seeing it as a burden, we must embrace it as an opportunity to showcase the exceptional performance and outcomes we see in our students and staff every day.

And if we find outcomes lacking, let's view it as a challenge to take action.

Scientific research has clearly and repeatedly demonstrated the link between school-wide PBS implementation and a decrease in classroom disruptions, office referrals, an increase in student achievement, and an improvement in school climate and safety — now it's your turn.

Our communities wants accountability - let's give them great results!

Preview

When someone tells us they are using this or that program, system, or method and things are going well, our first question should be, "How do you measure outcomes?"

Many people rely on their gut feelings, but we all know that this feeling is too subjective. Our yardstick for change must be reliable and valid measures.

Let's talk about how you can begin to measure your current school climate before you role out PBS. This is a pre-assessment and required to gain buy-in from staff. These tools help you answer the question: "Why is PBS needed here" that we asked in the Ownership chapter.

Additional standardised evaluation and fidelity instruments will be introduced in the KOI PBS Tier 2 Manual chapter titled Assessment - Tier 2 once you actually roll out or implement your PBS system.

Use a Data Audit Tool

A Data Audit Tool (DAT) is a summative evaluation tool that preserves four metrics (see Gallery):
- Academic Data - state test scores
- Behaviour/Discipline Data - ODR, OSS, expulsion, graduation, and drop-out rates
- Ethnic Disproportionality Data - total population, general ed., special ed., seclusion, and physical/mechanical restraint
- Special Education Data - referral and identification rates

With a DAT, school data are easily comparable over a 5 year period. We know you may have multiple databases where this information is stored, so this tool simply puts all the data on one spreadsheet to analyse trends in your data across domains and across time to see how the data interacts with each other.

If PBS is implemented with fidelity, you will see an increase in academic achievement scores, a decrease in office discipline referral data, suspensions and expulsions, as well as a decrease in special education referrals and eligibility. All this translates into a smart return on investment for professional development training.

Download the DAT spreadsheet (adapted from the Illinois PBIS Network Data Audit Tool) from koi-education.com/resources.

Parts of the Data Audit Tool (DAT)

Baseline and Year Columns
Baseline year is the year immediately before PBS implementation; Year 1 is the first year the complete school-wide system was rolled out.

Total Enrolment
Use your 100 day count for consistency across years.

Standardised Test Data
Use official results published by your state department of education for your school for consistency across years.

Behaviour Data
is always the total number for a given ethnic group. % is either percent of Total Enrolment at top of page or Percent of Incidents.

Enrolment by Race
Compare % enrolment by race against % incidents of ODR or Seclusion/Restraint. If there is greater then a 10% difference, then your discipline is disproportionate. See Data Analysis Chapter for more information on cultural responsibility.

Seclusion & Restraint

All public schools are currently required to report aggregate seclusion/restraint data

Special Education Data

Record the total number of students referred for testing and the number qualified for special education services annually.

Figure 4.1 Data Audit Tool

Download from KOI-education.com/resources.

Abbreviations:

 # - Number
% - Percent
ODR - Office Discipline Referral
ISS - In School Suspension
OSS - Out of School Suspension
Grad. - Graduation Rate
Total Pop. - Total population
Gen.Ed.Pop. - Total general education population
Sp.Ed.Pop. - Total special education population

Positive Behavior Interventions and Supports of Arizona
MULTI-TIERED SYSTEMS OF SUPPORT

DATA AUDIT TOOL (DAT)

The purpose of the DAT is to track PBIS outcomes

School Name	Sample Middle School		
District Name	Big District		
Contact Person	Calle Mea	Title	PBIS District Coordinator
Email	Calle.Mea@BigDistrict.com	Phone	123-456-7890
Type of School (choose)	Middle School		
	Public		

Notes
PBISaz DAT Adapted from the Illinois PBIS Network DAT.
Updated April 2015.

	Data Source	Type of Data	Baseline: 2018-2019 (Year 0 PBIS)
1.	100 Day Count from School	Total Enrollment	600

2. ADE Published Results (www.ade.az.gov)	Academic Standardized Test Data (add % Meets + % Exceeds Criteria)	2	3	4	5	6	7	8	9	10
	Reading					65	70	60		
	Writing/Language					70	72	65		
	Math					54	62	59		
	Science					66	71	55		

3. From School Database	Behavior Data (% is percent of total incidents)	ODR #	ODR %	ISS #	ISS %	OSS #	OSS %	Expulsion #	Expulsion %	Grad. #	Grad. %	DropOut #	DropOut %
	American Indian	200	22.60	18	26%	12	19%	0	0%	20	23%	2	13%
	Asian	120	14%	14	20%	1	2%	0	0%	9	10%	1	7%
	Black/African American	72	8%	12	17%	13	21%	0	0%	7	8%	2	13%
	Hispanic/Latino (Ethnicity)	23	3%	4	6%	2	3%	0	0%	7	8%	3	20%
	Pacific Islander/Hawaiian	0	0%	0	0%	0	0%	0	0%	0	0%	0	0%
	White	470	53%	22	31%	34	55%	3	100%	43	50%	7	47%
	Two or More Races	0	0%	0	0%	0	0%	0	0%	0	0%		0%
	Total (% is percent of enrollment)	885	100%	70	12%	62	10%	3	1%	86	14%	15	3%
	General Education Population	800	133%	40	6.7%	10	2%	0	0%		0%		0%
	Special Education Population	85	14%	20	3%	0	0%	0	0%		0%		0%

4. From School Database	Enrollment by Race (% is percent of total enrollment)	Total Pop #	Total Pop %	Gen.Ed. #	Gen.Ed. %	Sp.Ed. Pop #	Sp.Ed. Pop %
	American Indian	12	2%	7	1%	5	1%
	Asian	18	3%	18	3%	0	0%
	Black/African American	200	33%	175	29%	25	4%
	Hispanic/Latino (Ethnicity)	150	25%	142	24%	8	1%
	Pacific Islander/Hawaiian	5	1%	5	1%	0	0%
	White	215	36%	168	28%	47	8%
	Two or More Races	0	0%	0	0%	0	0%
	Total (% is percent of enrollment)	600	100%	515	86%	85	14%
	General Education Population	515	86%				
	Special Education Population	85	14%				

Abbreviations:

ODR = Office Discipline Referral
ISS = In School Suspension
OSS = Out of School Suspension
Grad = Graduation Rate (Gr.12)
Total Pop = Total Population
GenEd = General Education
SpEd = Special Education

Referred = Referred for a SpEd Evaluation
Qualified = Qualified for a SpEd Services

5. From School Database	Seclusion and Restraint (% is percent of total incidents)	Seclusion #	Seclusion %	Physical Restraint #	Physical Restraint %	Mechanical Restraint #	Mechanical Restraint %
	American Indian	0	0%	0	0%	0	DIV/0!
	Asian	0	0%	0	0%	0	DIV/0!
	Black/African American	3	100%	1	33%	0	DIV/0!
	Hispanic/Latino (Ethnicity)	0	0%	0	0%	0	DIV/0!
	Pacific Islander/Hawaiian	0	0%	0	0%	0	DIV/0!
	White	0	0%	2	67%	0	DIV/0!
	Two or More Races	0	0%	0	0%	0	DIV/0!
	Total (% is percent of enrollment)	3	1%	3	1%	0	0%
	General Education Population	0	0%	0	0%	0	0%
	Special Education Population	3	1%	3	1%	0	0%

6. From School Database	Special Education Data	Referred #	Referred %	Qualified #	Qualified %
	Total (% is percent of enrollment)	65	11%	50	8%

Referred = Referred for a SpEd Evaluation
Qualified = Qualified for a SpEd Service

Distribute Climate Surveys

Climate surveys are valuable for assessing the change in people's perception of the school's ambience and their feeling of safety. By measuring these qualitative perceptions, we can analyse if, over time, there is a quantitative change for the better with PBIS implementation. Climate surveys are designed to be collected annually from all school stakeholders. Initial survey results can be used to build ownership and buy-in by showing that there is a dire need for change. Future survey results can be compared to the early years to show PBIS's positive impact on school climate, equity, and safety.

PBIS climate surveys are completed online using the secure and free PBIS Assessment application within PBISapps.org (discussed later in this chapter). Each survey includes a set of demographic questions about the participant and several questions related to school climate with the Likert scale response option. The survey takes about 10–15 minutes to complete.

PBIS Assessment School Climate Surveys	
Elementary School Students	Provide schools with an overall understanding of how elementary students perceive school climate along four dimensions: school connectedness, school safety, school orderliness, and peer and adult relations
Middle School and High School Students	Provide schools with an overall understanding of how middle and secondary students perceive school climate along three dimensions: teaching and learning, relationships, and safety
School Personnel	Assesses the perception of staff along six dimensions: staff connectedness, structure for learning, physical environment, peer/adult relationships, and parent involvement
Family	Assesses the perception of families along five dimensions: teaching and learning, school safety, interpersonal relationships, institutional environment, and parent involvement

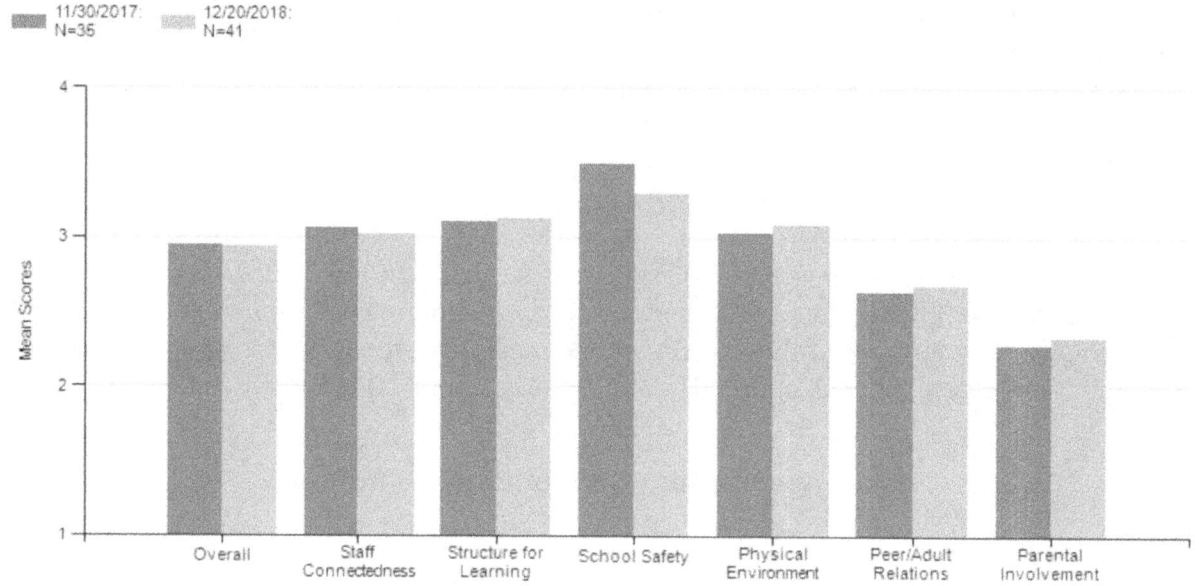

N=Number of respondents

A little pre-planning goes a long way when it comes to distributing and analysing climate data.

1. Schedule the survey window (when the survey will be open and available) for 1 week and schedule when results will be shared with each stakeholder group. Then plan the promotion of the survey (announcements, print, digital) accordingly.
2. Ask your local PBIS Assessment coordinator (covered later in this chapter) to open the surveys in PBISapps and share the unique URL link for each group of participants with the PBIS team.
3. Plan to share these links in an easily accessible location such as your school website, staff email/meeting, social media post, or newsletters.
4. Ask your local PBIS Assessment coordinator to close the surveys at the end of the window and share the results with the team.
5. Results (good, bad, and ugly) must be shared with all stakeholders within 1–2 weeks of collecting data in order to build trust with the PBIS team.

Tips and Strategies for Success

Each stakeholder group requires a different approach in order to collect the most accurate results possible.

Students
- Pre-readers in grades K-2 can be asked as a group by their teacher for their response to each survey question, which can then be entered by their classroom teacher.
- New or struggling readers can have the survey read to them by an adult, question-by-question.
- Designate 5-10 minutes from one common class period to collect results: homeroom, English, or period 1 classes.
- Consider piloting the survey with 1-3 teachers before the survey window opens to identify if special instructions are needed or to assess how easy it was to find/access the survey link.

School Personnel
- Assure staff that the survey is 100% anonymous and their name is never going to be connected to the results even if they are signed into a school computer.
- Ensure that all the staff are given the opportunity to submit feedback: teachers, support personnel and aides, administrative assistance, before/after school staff, etc.
- The best response rate is attained when 10-15 minutes is designated at a scheduled staff or department meeting. Relying on people to find the time to click a link in one of the 100 emails received each week is not recommended.

Families
- Share the link using multiple modalities: Email newsletters, paper notes home, social media channels. Post videos promoting the survey, ask students to make signs, and turn this into an event!
- Consider collecting family surveys in conjunction with other school events such as parent-teacher conferences, football/basketball or sporting events, or school performance or celebration. Set up computers for easy access and add raffle drawings to encourage participation.

Poor Survey Response Rate?

A poor survey response rate may be an indication of a climate of apathy at the school – or just bad timing, organization, or dissemination glitches. Learn from the experience and make it better the following year. Use an increase in response rates each year as one factor that indicates that your school climate, safety, and feelings of equity are improving. Promote the positive subscales to show what a great school you have and why staff, students, and families want to be a part of your community - connect school climate to your PBIS expectations and values.

Collect Testimonial Data

Have you ever impulsively bought a product from an infomercial or based on an advertisement? Many of us have been persuaded!

The Power of Persuasion

We often make decisions based on our heart (emotion) and not our head (reason). Even though PBS is an evidence-based practice supported by scientific experimentation at tens of thousands of schools for over a decade, it's often a person saying, "This worked for me last year!" that persuades people to give it a try.

Testimonials are important when you are building staff ownership and buy-in. If you skip the Ownership building process, research shows that you are less likely to achieve fidelity (people actually implementing PBS correctly once it's implemented) and less likely to see outcomes (decreased referrals, increased achievement, or improved climate).

View and share videos as examples of school personnel sharing their perceptions of PBS and the outcomes they personally experienced.

Testimonial Tips

Even if your school has never implemented PBS before, staff who have worked at other schools, districts, or states may have direct experience with PBS systems or may know of people who use it to deliver exemplary outcomes. Ask around and ask colleagues to help you spread the word!

Ask for written or video testimonials (30-60 seconds) from staff, students, or parents discussing your current school climate and why it is not as positive as it could be. Hearing negative comments from parents, students or colleagues about your school will often convey the fact that there is a real need for change! This can be much more convincing than hearing it from an administrator or outside expert.

Share these videos with staff or create your own if you know someone who has had a positive experience with PBS.

 **Movie 4.1 Pioneer Elementary School**
Becky Rusher shares a testimonial about how PBS has impacted staff and students at her school.
View at vimeo.com/59356452

Utilise PBISapps.org

What Is PBISapps?

PBISapps is a website with a suite of tools and databases for monitoring and graphing the effectiveness of PBS at schools, across a state, or around the nation. The website also has tools for monitoring targeted behaviour programs such as Check-In/Check-Out and individual student behaviour interventions. Dr. Robert Horner and colleagues created the website at the University of Oregon as part of a federal grant for PBS research that began in 1998. Dr. Horner, Dr. Sugai and Dr. Lewis were the initial co-directors of the National Technical Assistance Center on Positive Behavior Supports (PBIS.org). This is a collaboration between the U.S. Department of Education and more than a dozen other universities across the U.S. In 2018, the Center earned it's fifth 5-year grant to continue funding research on PBS.

The research at PBIS.org "focuses on the development and implementation of practices that result in positive, durable, and scientifically validated change in the lives of individuals with disabilities and their families" (Retrieved August 1, 2013 from PBISapps.org/About-Us).

Is PBISapps Secure?

School and student data are very safe! Data is stored on a secure server at the University of Oregon utilizing the latest digital security encryption. (It can also be stored at a university in your country, outside of the US.) Aggregated data is used for research purposes, but only after requests have been submitted and approved by a university Institutional Review Board (IRB). Schools can only see their own data. Local coordinators can see data for schools they coordinate - this is necessary so they can do their job to assist you in entering and analysing your data.

Why Do Schools Need PBISapps?

There are two databases that schools regularly access from PBISapps:

PBIS Assessment:
Free: PBIS Assessment includes several surveys that a school team can use to self-assess the components of a multi-tiered PBS system that are present or absent in their school. Different surveys are used to answer different questions. Results are automatically graphed and can be used to action plan the changes needed to increase fidelity and outcomes for the school. All surveys are evidence-based, valid/reliable, and have published psychometric properties. See Gallery images. The PBIS Assessments Users Manual is available to download at any time from the PBISapps Resources page.

SWIS Suite:

Fee Based: This suite of tools includes a database for entering all office discipline referral (ODR) data which it then automatically graphs and displays on a dashboard. In addition to the 'Big 7' most frequently viewed graphs, schools can easily filter data and drill-down to look at dozens of pre-made graphs or custom sort based on need.

Get PBIS Assessment

Access to PBIS Assessment is provided through a local PBS Assessment Coordinator who can apply to PBISapps for your free account. Your Coordinator will open/close surveys for schools and provide access to each school so you can enter survey data and view reports from your school. You can easily view graphs and tables of your survey data anytime or even compare results across years.

Two ways to gain access to PBIS Assessment:
1. If you are training with KOI Education, we are your PBS Assessment Coordinator and will set up your account. Then we will teach you how to be your own Coordinator.
2. If you are not training with KOI Education, you can contact us to help you, find a local Coordinator near you at PBISapps.org, or someone in your school district can apply to be the local Coordinator for your district schools. We can provide all the training you need or you can spend the time to teach yourself using PBISapps manuals and videos.

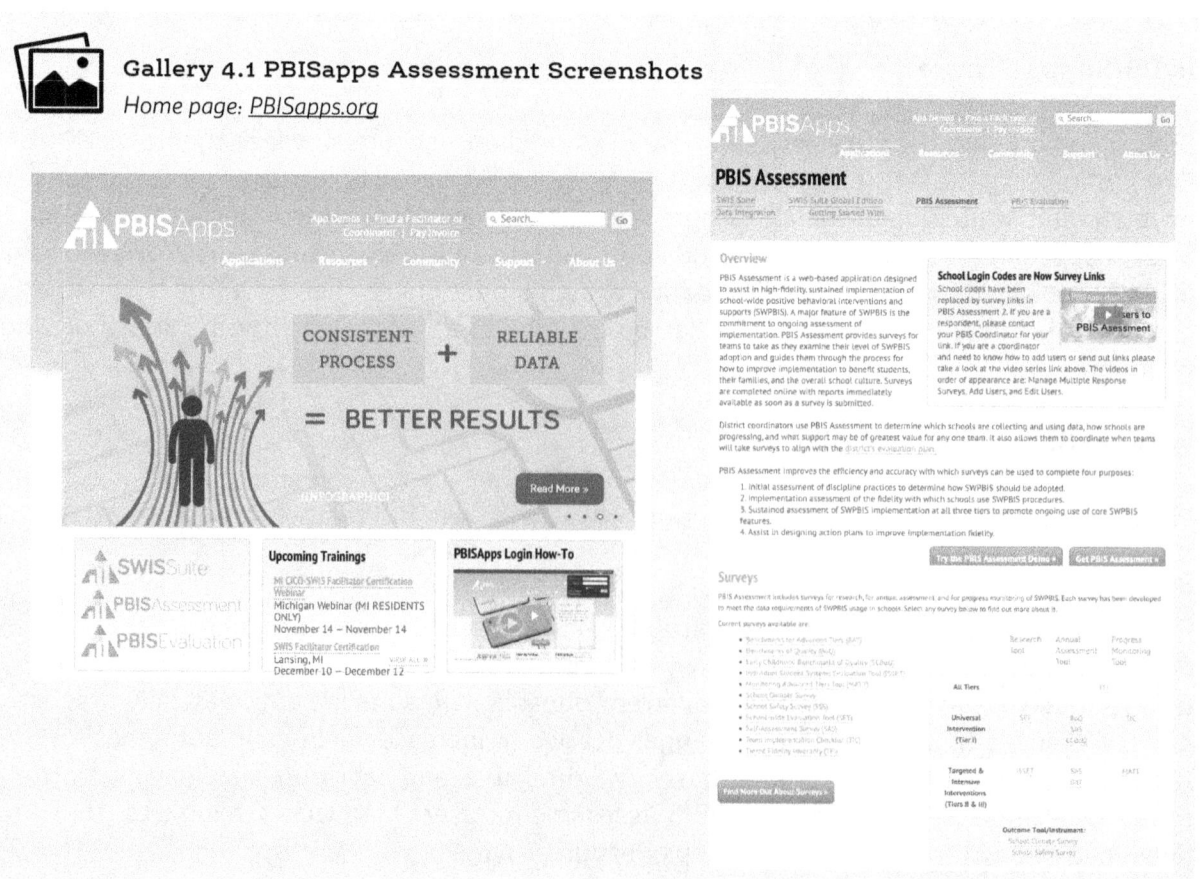

Gallery 4.1 PBISapps Assessment Screenshots
Home page: PBISapps.org

PBIS Assessment Surveys

PBIS Assessment offers so many surveys that it can be a daunting process to choose the right tool for the job. It's important to remember that schools do not need to use all the surveys every year. Check with your trainer and external coach to choose the surveys that give you the answers you need to make decisions that increase your effectiveness.

The following surveys can be used to assess Tier 1 implementation fidelity: TFI & SAS.

TFI: Tiered Fidelity Inventory

The TFI is the newest PBISapps survey. It allows a school to self-assess one or all three tiers of their PBS systems. Having one tool to survey all tiers of a PBS system is appealing because it is all-inclusive.

However, this also makes the TFI much broader in scope because there are only 15 elements/questions per tier - much less feedback then the TIC or BOQ for Tier 1. It is recommended that the TFI be completed with a trained external coach for best results since this survey requires documents and 'proof' of implementation when used correctly. The TFI requires a 'Walkthrough Tool' for Tier 1 and a 'Behaviour Support Plan Worksheet' for Tier 3 be completed before a PBS team can answer all survey questions.

Gallery 4.2 Screenshot of TFI Graphs

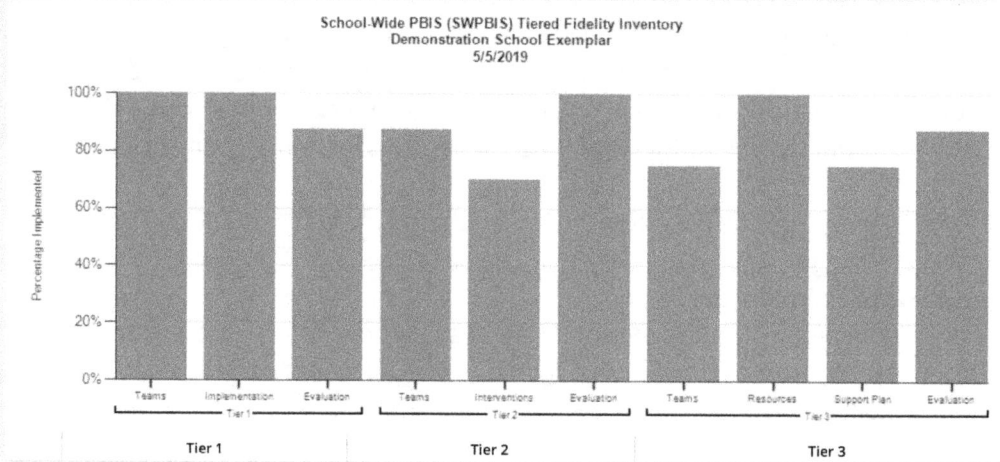

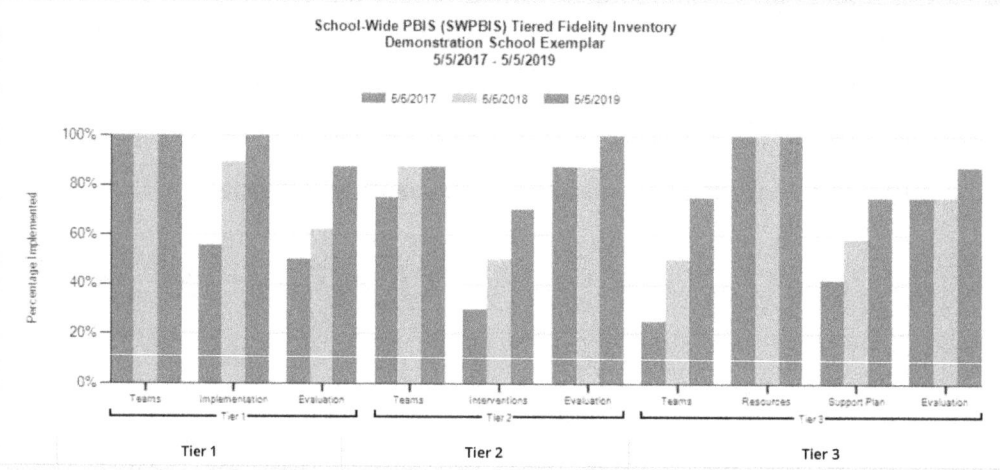

SAS: Self-Assessment Survey
Schools can use this Self-Assessment Survey "to identify the staff perception of the implementation status and improvement priority for school-wide, classroom, non-classroom and individual student systems" (Retrieved August 1, 2013 from PBISapps.org).

The results of the survey can be used to:
- Action plan
- Make implementation changes
- Assess staff perception of implementation status & priority
- Validate team perception of implementation status & priority
- Monitor positive change across years

The survey will take staff approximately 20 minutes to complete, so scheduling and providing adequate time will increase participation and thoughtful answers. Staff are asked to rate all 36 school features for Current Status (in place, partially in place, or not in place) as well as Priority for Improvement (high, medium, low).

When all staff have entered their opinions, you must ask your PBS Assessment Coordinator to close the survey before you can see the results. Teams can view results by total score, sub-scale, or items and download as a PDF file to share with staff.

It is extremely important to interpret and share results with staff after they generously shared their opinions and their time. This builds trust with the PBS team and promotes a positive school climate.

Process
1. Login to PBISapps.org.
2. Locate the 'Self-Assessment Survey', select 'Link', and copy/share the URL link provided with your staff.
3. Ask PBS Coordinator to close the SAS when staff have finished taking the survey.
4. Select 'Reports' to see graphed results.

Gallery 4.3 Screenshot of SAS

	Current Status				Priority for Improvement			
	In Place	Partial In Place	Not In Place	Don't Know/NA	High	Med	Low	Don't Know/NA
1. A small number (e.g. 3-5) of positively & clearly stated student expectations or rules are defined.	○	○	○	●	○	○	○	●
2. Expected student behaviors are taught directly.	○	○	○	●	○	○	○	●
3. Expected student behaviors are rewarded regularly.	○	○	○	●	○	○	○	●
4. Problem behaviors (failure to meet expected student behaviors) are defined clearly.	○	○	○	●	○	○	○	●
5. Consequences for problem behaviors are defined clearly.	○	○	○	●	○	○	○	●
6. Distinctions between office v. classroom managed problem behaviors are clear.	○	○	○	●	○	○	○	●

Reflection

Take a minute to reflect on all the assessments tools:
Which of the assessment tools are you most interested in using—why?
What purpose does each tool serve?

Action Plan

1. Contact a local PBS Assessment Coordinator to access PBISapps (your KOI Trainer/Coach is your Coordinator)
2. Complete the Data Audit Tool (Quantitive)
3. Distribute the PBISapps.org climate surveys (Qualitative)
4. Collect Testimonials (Anecdotal)
5. Complete the TFI with the PBIS Tier 1 team and coach
6. Schedule time to analyse then share TFI results/growth with staff
7. Schedule time for all school staff to complete the SAS. Send staff the 'Link'. Close survey before viewing results.
8. Schedule time to interpret and share SAS results with staff

Resources

- Data Audit Tool (DAT)
- PBISapps.org Climate Surveys for Student, Staff, and Families
- PBISapps.org for PBIS Assessment surveys (TFI, SAS)

Available from koi-education.com/resources

Evaluation

1. The Data Audit Tool collects data from all these sources except:
   a. Attendance Data
   b. Special Education Data
   c. Behaviour Data
   d. Academic Data

2. What are the benefits of online Climate Surveys:
   a. Save time - no need to enter data by hand
   b. Save money - no need to photocopy papers
   c. Save work—easy to copy/paste results and share outcomes
   d. All of the above

3. People usually make decisions with their:
   a. Head—using reason
   b. Heart—using emotion

4. How can schools access PBISapps Surveys?
   a. Sign up with your Facebook ID
   b. Create a fake account
   c. Download the app for your smartphone
   d. Ask your KOI Education Trainer or local PBS Assessment Coordinator for access.

5. What surveys should be completed using PBISapps in the first quarter of school?
   a. DAT
   b. Climate Surveys
   c. SAS
   d. TIC
   e. A and B
   f. C and D

6. What surveys cannot be completed on PBISapps?
   a. DAT
   b. Climate Surveys
   c. TFI
   d. SAS

Answers: 1a, 2d, 3b, 4d, 5f, 6a

Chapter 5
Expectation System

CHOOSE EXPECTATIONS
THAT REFLECT THE CULTURE
YOU WANT TO PROMOTE.

Expectation System

Learning Objectives

Identify School-Wide Expectations

Identify School Locations

Identify Rules/Skills for Each Expectation and Location

 Movie 5.1 Expectation Introduction

Dr. Jannasch-Pennell discusses the similarities between creating academic expectations and behaviour or social expectations. View at http://youtu.be/mY81ARHC-XU

Preview

We set expectations for our students in reading, writing, math, the arts, and sports. However, we rarely set expectations for behaviour.

We often assume that students will learn the correct way to behave in school through osmosis or that they must know what I mean when I say "Be Respectful" - even though every person has a different definition and picture in their head of what "Respectful" may look like.

It's time to **stop** making assumptions!

Identify School-Wide Expectations

Select 3-4 School-Wide Expectations

Choosing school-wide expectations should involve as many staff, students, and parents as possible. Expectations should reflect the culture that you want to create at your school. The more ownership and buy-in achieved at this stage, the easier it will be to implement these new expectations when you roll out your complete PBS system.

The 'Word Cloud' in the Gallery illustrates some of the most common expectations found across the country. In a word cloud, the larger the word, the more frequently it appears in school PBS systems. You can create your own word cloud at wordle.net.

Tips:
- Do: Choose 3-4 expectations that fit the values and behaviours you want to see from your students, staff and families
- Don't: Pick words just because they fit an acronym or the initials for your school (PAWS, ROAR, PRIDE, GPA

High School). You may end up doing verbal acrobatics to find a word that fits, but does not match the values or traits that reflect the culture of your school.
- Read On: Each Expectation still needs to be defined in each location of the school. Ask if each Expectation makes sense in the restroom/toilet area!

See more examples of expectations throughout this chapter. All documents and examples at koi-education.com/resources.

Gallery 5.1 Expectation Wordle
Sample of expectations from over 100 schools. Most frequent expectations appear the largest. Created with www.wordle.net

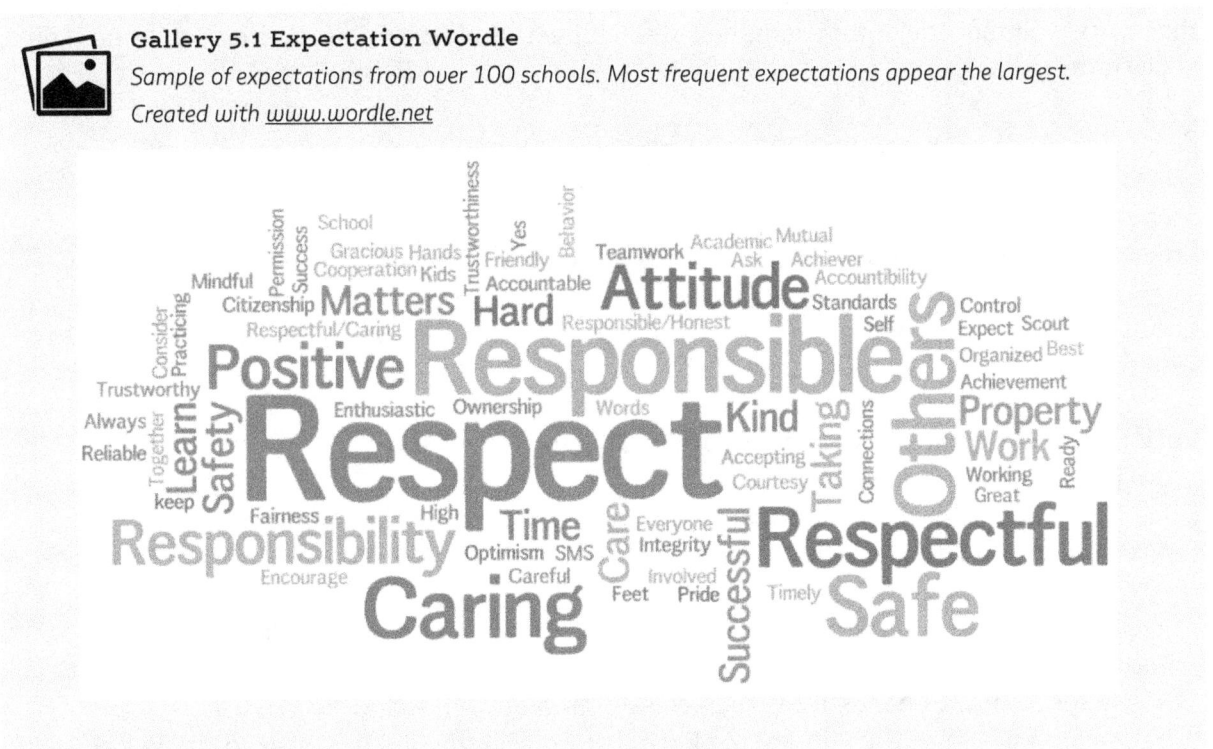

Brainstorm Process

We recommend a four-step process with your staff or a large group of stakeholders to narrow down expectations, values and traits from a world of possibilities - but the final vote must be with your entire community to generate buy-in and ownership:

Step 1:
Individually and silently brainstorm 3-6 expectations/values/traits per person and write each one on a sticky-note.

Place sticky-notes on a wall/window, consolidating similar words into columns to make a bar graph of expectations.

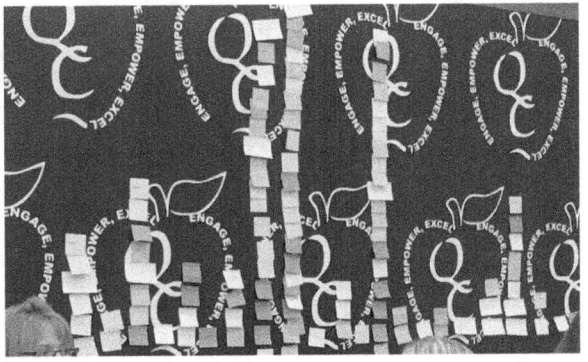

Step 2:
Provide 4-6 sticker dots per person, place a dot on your favourite expectations (it may not be the most popular word)

Choose 10-15 expectations with the most dots (most popular).

Step 3:
In small groups, sort popular expectations (from step 2) into bundles of 3-4 expectations that work well together - for example: Safe, Respectful, Responsible. Write each bundle on a sticky-note.

Place sticky-notes on a wall/window (1-2 bundles per group).

Step 4:
Provide 1-2 sticker dots per person, place a dot on your favourite bundle.

Choose the 3 bundles with the most dots (most popular) - ask your school community to vote for their favourite expectations.

Vote on Expectations - Keep the Voting Simple

Once your team/school brainstorms expectations that reflect the culture you want at your school, put it to a vote. Options:

- Give everyone (staff/students/families) a ballot to put in a box labelled with three expectation choices
- Ask for a show of hands from each class or at a staff meeting
- Use an online poll such as Google Forms or Poll Daddy and post the voting link on a website or your social media pages.

The more staff, students and families involved in the brainstorm and voting process, the more buy-in, ownership and trust is developed in your PBS team.

Brand It!

Once you choose your expectations, be sure to 'Brand It' and create a name for your expectations - for example:
- 3 B's - Be Respectful, Be Responsible and Be Safe
- CR2 Expectations - Be Caring, Respectful and Responsible
- Lincoln School Pact - Respectful, Responsible and Kind

Branding makes it possible to teach and remember your expectations easily . Even a visitor to campus can ask staff or students, "What are the 3B's?" and can be answered quickly and easily. Or a staff member can ask a student, "What do the 3B's look like in the Cafeteria?" or "Is that 3B's behaviour? No? Tell me what 3B's we expect to see in the classroom with a substitute or casual relief teacher".

Gallery 5.2 Branded Expectations
Branding your Expectations make them personal and easy to remember!

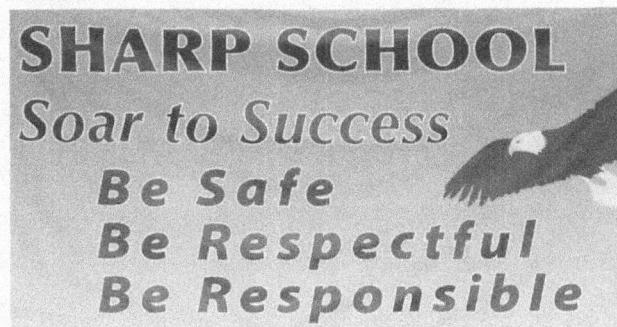

Reflection

Take a minute to reflect on creating expectations.
Why create common school-wide behaviour expectations?
Who should we include in creating expectations?

Identify School Locations

Select 4–6 locations around the school where the expectations need to be defined differently

Identifying locations ensures that students know what is expected of them in the different areas of campus. The purpose is to be proactive and prevent behaviour problems. For example, "Respect" in the classroom may be defined as "use an inside voice", but on the playground or sports field "Respect" is "use school appropriate language". (This will be covered in the next section).

- Choose too few locations and the rules may not generalise.
- Choose too many locations and no one will be able to remember all the different rules for the expectations.

Here are some locations that need to be considered:
- Classroom
- Hallway/walkways
- Restroom/toilet
- Cafeteria
- Playground/recess/recreation area/sports venue
- Common areas
- Bus

See pictures of Expectations in different locations in the Gallery.

Gallery 5.3 Expectation in Different Locations

Play

Hall

Toilet

Outdoors

Identify Skills/Rules for Each Expectation and Location

Guideline for Choosing Skills

- Skills must be stated positively - tell students what you want them to do:
    - Instead of yelling, "Don't run!", we should state, "walk".
    - Instead of demanding, "No hitting or kicking", remind students to, "Keep hands, feet, and objects to yourself".
- Skills must be specific and observable
- Skills must be concrete examples of the expectations
- Review office referral data to identify the most problematic behaviours on campus or in a certain location - be sure to include all essential skills you expect on your matrix

See Gallery 5.4 for an Expectations Skills/Rules document with dozens of positively worded skills/rules. See Gallery 5.5 for completed Expectation Matrix example.

Remember to work with your bus transportation department to ensure that bus rules are stated positively and taught to students by the drivers several times per year. The Positive Bus Safety System (PBISS) from KOI Education is a complete process for developing an Expectation Matrix, Lesson Plans, Reinforcement Matrix, Behaviour Flowchart and Bus Evacuation Lesson Plan with the transportation leadership team.

Gallery 5.4 Expectation Skills/Rules Examples
Download from koi-education.com/resources.

Classroom	Hallway	Playground/Recess
•Always do your best	•Use the correct door	•Use kind words to others
•Be on task	•Walk on the right	•Involve everyone
•Be cooperative	•Keep hands and feet to yourself	•Share equipment
•Follow adults directions	•Inside voices	•Follow game's rules
•Keep hands, feet and objects to yourself	•Hold door open for others	•Listen and follow adult directions
•Share/help others	•Pick up trash	•Keep hands and feet to yourself
•Use inside voice	•Turn in lost items to the office	•Use equipment properly
•Recycle	•Walk quietly	•Put equipment back into place
•Clean up after yourself	•Be on time	•Take turns
•Take care of your own belongings	•Allow others to pass	•Defend victim being bullied
•Be polite	•Greet others politely	•Ask aids for help
•Put materials away	•Listen and follow directions	•Play nicely
•Be prepared	•Close lockers gently	•Think safety
•Follow instructions	•Keep hallways clean	•Use your time wisely
•Raise your hand	•Head directly to your destination	•Head back to classroom on time
•Listen to others	•Pay attention when walking	•Keep area clean
•Stay in the classroom	•Make sure to have a pass	
•Think before you act	•Walking only	
•Use appropriate language	•Keep our walls clean	
•Keep pets at home		
•Have homework completed by the time school starts		
•Accept consequences for your actions		

Limit the Number of Skills/Rules Per Location

Too many skills can be overwhelming:

3 Expectations X 5 Locations X 3 Skill = 45 Skills
5 Expectations X 5 Locations X 3 Skill = 75 Skills!!!

Expectation Checklist
- ✔ Brand It!
- ✔ School Mascot or Logo
- ✔ Use positive language
- ✔ Use specific/observable language
- ✔ Use identical words/phrase for identical ideas
- ✔ Keep repeated skills under the same expectation
- ✔ List repeated skills first in each location

Double Check
Confirm with your staff that your Expectations and Skills/Rules make sense. Pretend to acknowledge a student for meeting the Expectations or hold them accountable when they are not meeting the Expectations.
- "Thank you for Expectation by Skill!"
- "What does it look like to be Expectation in Location?"

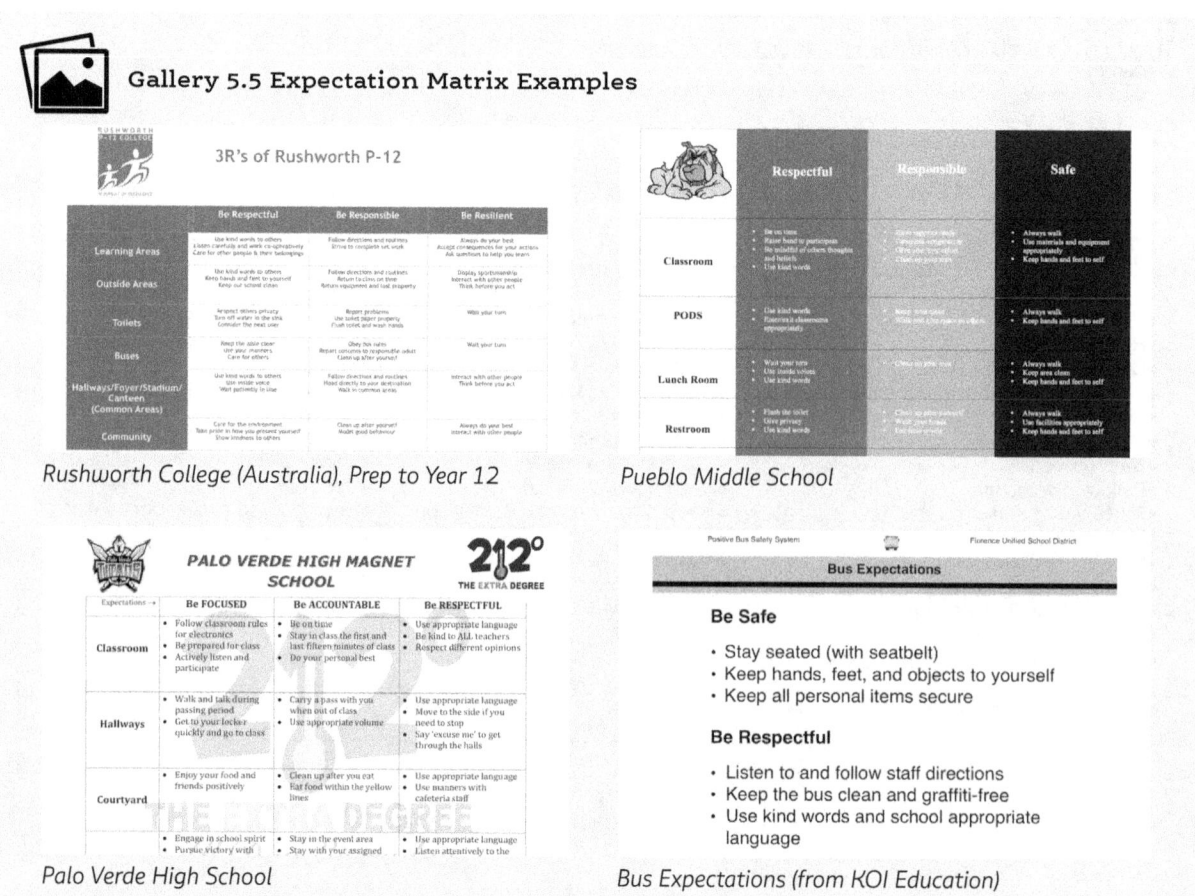

Gallery 5.5 Expectation Matrix Examples

Rushworth College (Australia), Prep to Year 12

Pueblo Middle School

Palo Verde High School

Bus Expectations (from KOI Education)

Reflection

Why state skills positively?
What skills do you need to remind students about most frequently in your classroom?

Action Plan

1. Create 3 bundles/choices of 3-4 school-wide Expectations to present to the staff and students for a vote.
2. Choose locations and skills/rules to create an Expectation Matrix.

Resources

- Expectation Matrix (Template)
- Expectation Matrix Examples
- Expectation Wordle
- Expectation Skills/Rules

Available from koi-education.com/resources.

Evaluation

1. How many expectations are recommended?
   a. 1
   b. 3
   c. 6
   d. As many as you wish!

2. What locations are recommended for posting expectations?
   a. Classrooms
   b. Hallways
   c. Bathrooms
   d. Bus
   e. All of the above

3. Should school rules should be abstract and very general?
   a. Yes
   b. No

4. Which is not listed on the Expectation Checklist?
   a. Use positive language
   b. List repeated skills first in each location
   c. Use identical words/phrases for identical ideas
   d. List 4-6 skills per Expectation in each location

Answers: 1b, 2e, 3b, 4d

Chapter 6
Teaching System

WE TEACH READING, WRITING, MATH AND SPORTS SKILLS.

WHY NOT TEACH SOCIAL BEHAVIOUR SKILLS?

Teaching System

Learning Objectives

Assess Where to Display Expectations

Create Lesson Plans for Staff and Students

Schedule Training for Staff and Students

 Movie 6.1 Teaching Introduction

Dr. Flores reminds us that behaviour is a skill, just like reading, writing, math, and sports. It can be taught. View at http://youtu.be/SRVYabOfUF0

Preview

Behaviour is a skill just like reading, writing, trigonometry or driving a car. Thus, behaviour must be learned and is acquired through practice.

It is essential to teach school-wide social and behaviour expectations before expecting students or staff to demonstrate these skills correctly - teaching first, expect second.

Assess Where to Display Expectations

Expectations need to be visible in all locations of a school if we want staff and students to learn to use them consistently.

Of course, just posting expectation alone does about as much for teaching behaviour as posting the grammar rules does for teaching writing or posting the Periodic Table does for teaching chemistry.

It is a visual reminder and reference tool, and it is only effective after the expectations have been taught and reinforced.

Poster Checklist

- Branding
- Location
- Expectations
- Skills/Rules

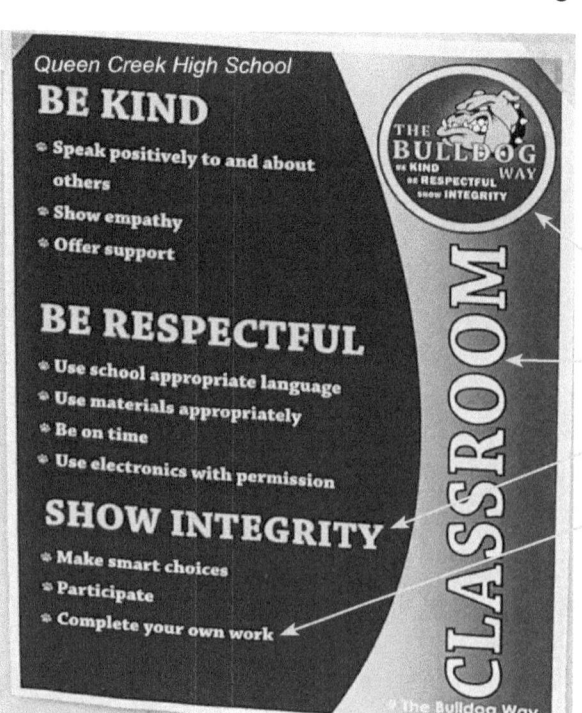

Four Choices to Make When Posting Expectations

1) Size
- The poster must be readable from across the room - different sizes for different spaces (bathroom, classroom, cafeteria, etc.).
- Suggestions: 8" x 12" in bathrooms, 2' x 3' in classrooms, 6' x 12' in cafeteria.
- Print the expectations and skills for a specific location only (i.e.. Just the classroom expectations and rules/skills in the classroom).

2) Materials
- Enlarged photocopy or student created poster
- Painted poster or painted wall/walkway
- Vinyl banner

3) Cost
- Butcher or poster paper and paint may be cheap, but laminated posters and banners are more durable. Consider if you want to create posters annually or monthly!
- Create 10-20% more than needed so that when a poster rips, tears, or gets damaged, it can be replaced quickly.

4) Variety of Media
- Printing posters and banners for the school is important, but so is posting and promoting your PBS expectations more broadly.
- Consider flyers, newsletters, postcards and other ways of increasing the visibility and awareness of your school-wide expectations.
- Consider digital publishing and marketing of your school-wide expectations on your school website and social media channels.

Gallery 6.1 Expectations Posters
Only display the Expectations for the location where the poster is posted.

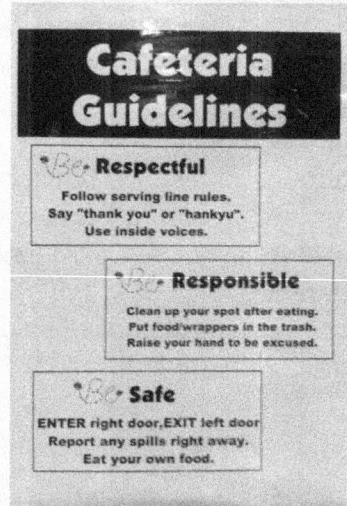
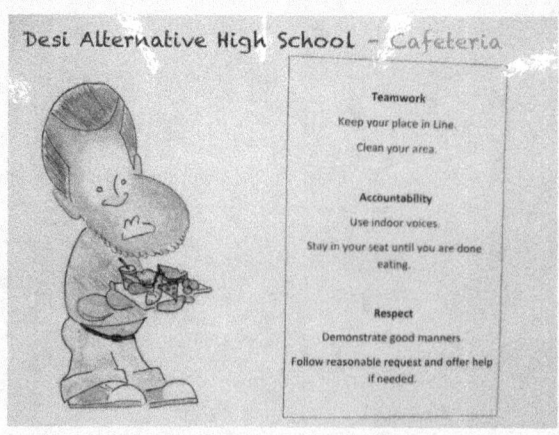

See Figure 6.1 for a handy Expectation Display Checklist.

Use the Expectation Display Checklist for planning and tracking the posters that need to be created - you may be surprised at the number and variety you need.

Figure 6.1 Display Expectations Checklist

Poster Location (Listing Expectations & Skills for that location)	Total #
Classroom/Labs/Library/Learning Area	
Bathroom	
Hall/Corridor/Walkway	
Cafeteria	
Auditorium/Gym	
Office	
Playground/Fields/Basketball Court	
Buses	
Other Area (list)	
Other Area (list)	
Other Area (list)	
Other Area (list)	
Total	

Banner Location (Listing Expectations only)	Total #
Front of School	
Gym	
Cafeteria	
Playground/Sport Field Fence	
Other Area (list)	
Other Area (list)	
Total	

> # Reflection
>
> *Take a minute to reflect on displaying expectations.*
> *Why is it important to brand your expectations?*
> *Why display the expectations and skills*
> *for each location in those locations?*

Create Lesson Plans for Staff and Students

Teaching social behaviour skills should follow the same effective strategies we use for teaching academic skills. We need to identify the objective, create a set or hook, and systematically take our students through the "I do, We do, You do" process. Then we need to evaluate if learners met our objective for the lesson.

Lesson Plan Template for Students

We suggest using a Lesson Plan template for consistency when teaching Expectations in all locations. This template is based on an example provided by Langland, S., Lewis-Palmer, T., & Sugai, G. (1998). The five sections are:

1. List the skills/rules for this Expectation in this Location from Expectation Matrix/Poster
2. List a rationale for teaching the behaviour (Why is it important?)
3. Identify examples and non-examples of the desired behaviour (What would the behaviour look/sound like? What would the behaviour not look/sound like?)
4. Practice/Role Play Activities
5. Provide opportunities for practice

Remember to create a lesson plan for each Expectation in each Location. One Expectation typically includes 3–4 skills/rules for each location. If a single lesson plan was created for; Be Respectful, Responsible, and Safe in the Classroom, that could total 12 or more rules/skills. Most teachers would never teach more than 2-3 objectives per academic lesson, so social/behaviour lessons should follow the same logic.

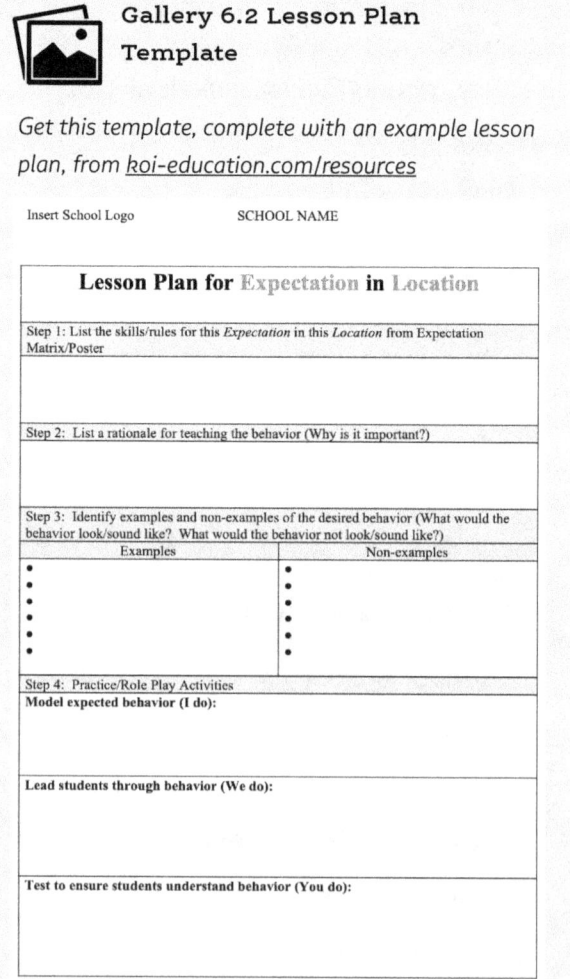

Gallery 6.2 Lesson Plan Template

Get this template, complete with an example lesson plan, from koi-education.com/resources

Video Lesson Plans

Watch some videos (Movie 6.2 - 6.5) from PBS schools and identify the following:

- Parts of the lesson plan template the school did well.
- Parts of the lesson plan template that could be improved or demonstrated more succinctly.

Movie 6.2 Jefferson Middle School Hip Tip #6 Hallway Behaviour
http://youtu.be/i3ywmqKN8dM

Movie 6.3 Durango High School
http://youtu.be/KGuYmUoP-9Q

Movie 6.4 1-2-3 Dancing Expectations – Franklin Elementary
http://vimeo.com/20955727

Movie 6.5 Bathroom Expectations - Mark Twain Elementary
http://youtu.be/Qqd1ePxG9N8

Movie 6.6 High School Hallway Expectations
https://youtu.be/wVLcEDJKy6E

Movie 6.7 High School Bathroom Expectations
https://youtu.be/26u1WLrSFTw

Making PBS Videos

Searching for good quality PBS videos is a daunting process via YouTube or other search sites. Our recommendation is to visit BET-C.org/awards and PBISvideos.com for a juried selection of videos submitted as part of PBS film festivals.

Consider submitting your school video to the national Association for Positive Behaviour Support (APBIS.org) PBS film festival each January!

Lesson Plans for Staff

Do not assume that staff know how to use an Expectation Matrix!

Lesson plans for staff can be created using the same format as student lesson plans, but should be developmentally appropriate—naturally.

When creating lesson plans for staff consider the scarcity of time typically allotted to professional development training and consider how to train staff who are not present during the initial whole-staff training.

Reflection

Take a minute to reflect on the creation and use of video lessons. What are the benefits of creating PBS videos for teaching your Expectation system to staff and students?

Schedule Training for Staff and Students

Consider Who, What, When, Where, and How training will occur at your school. There are many choices available! We recommend that staff is trained before the school year begins and students are trained the first week of the school year.

Who
Who will teach the lessons? PBS leadership team, administrators, teachers or students?

What
What will be taught? All expectations for all location at once, all expectations for one location at a time, all expectations and reinforcement and accountability systems at one time, daily lessons, or first day of each week?

When
When will training occur? During special events, a selected class period every day in the opening week, a selected period each week for an opening month, or each week the school can focus on a different expectation or location?

Where
Where will training occur? In an assembly, homeroom, in each location or online?

How
How will the training occur? A live event, lecture, slideshow, video or trivia game format?

Build your Teaching System with Sustainability in Mind

We never teach academic skills or a new skill only one time and expect students or adults to be 100% competent. There are natural phases of learning from acquisition to fluency to maintenance to generalisation. It takes time and repetition to learn any skill.

We can easily predict that there will never be 100% attendance at a training, and even if we achieve that, staff and students come and go from a school all the time. A system that is replicable and durable must be created.

For example:
>Performing a skit at monthly assemblies to reteach expectations is probably not feasible. But, we can video the skit or create a movie so that the content is reusable.

>Presentation slides and trivia games are additional examples of durable and reproducible training aids.

Reflection

Take a minute to reflect on scheduling training for your school-wide expectations. What are some creative ways that you can teach the Expectation Matrix to your staff and students?

Action Plan

1. Create, print and post the expectations in each school location.
2. Create lesson plans for each expectation in each location.
3. Schedule training for staff and students.

Resources

- Lesson Plan Template & Example
- Display Expectation Checklist

Available from koi-education.com/resources.

Evaluation

1. Why is it important to 'Brand' your Expectation Matrix?
   a. To compete with Nike—Just Do It
   b. To make a catchy jingle
   c. To teach capitalism, commercialism and bring in advertising revenue
   d. To instil a common language across the school

2. Video lesson plans for staff and students add efficiency because they are reusable:
   a. True
   b. False

3. Expectations can be taught:
   a. Online
   b. Via game show format
   c. By administration, staff, or students
   d. All at once or over time
   e. All of the above

Answers: 1d, 2a, 3e

Chapter 7
Reinforcement System

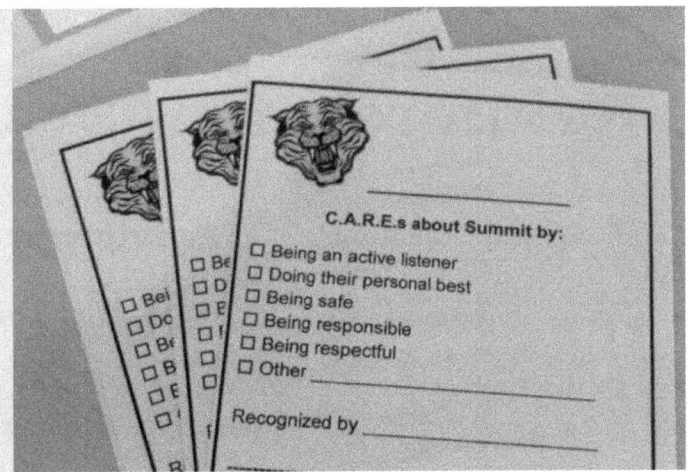

"IF YOU WANT CHILDREN TO IMPROVE, LET THEM OVERHEAR THE NICE THINGS YOU SAY ABOUT THEM."

—HAIM G. GINOTT

Reinforcement System

Learning Objectives

Address Reinforcement Myths

Create a Four Part Reinforcement Matrix

Teach the Reinforcement System to Staff and Students

Advanced Reinforcement Strategies

 Movie 7.1 Reinforcement Introduction

Dr. Gulchak and Dr. Flores role play the 3-Second / 3-Step reinforcement system—twice!

View at http://youtu.be/_FLLQIuGk80

Preview

Correct Academic and Social Behaviour

What typically happens when students demonstrate correct academic behaviour? That is, what happens when the subject matter that you have taught, rehearsed and provided feedback on has been demonstrated and mastered by your students? Typically, students are told their answer is correct, awarded an A+, given a happy face sticker, the teacher smiles or provides praise with a nod or thumbs up.

As educators we do this so students know the correct skill we are expecting, so in the future that skill can be demonstrated again.

In regards to social behaviour, what typically happens when students demonstrate correct social behaviours? Often nothing. We say it's expected! Why are we OK with acknowledging and reinforcing correct academic behaviours, but often don't acknowledge or reinforce correct social behaviours?

Incorrect Academic and Social Behaviour

What typically happens when students demonstrate incorrect academic behaviour? Do we send them to the office each time? No. We provide corrective feedback, we re-teach and provide opportunities to practice. Why? So students learn the correct skill and can demonstrate it in the future.

What typically happens when students demonstrate incorrect social behaviour? Often students are reprimanded, given a consequence (punishment), and sometimes exclusionary practices are used (time out, detention, office discipline referral, suspension).

In many schools there is a disconnect between how we address academic vs. social behaviours.

We want to teach social behavioural skills as we do academic skills. When correct/appropriate behaviours occur, we should recognise and reinforce the behaviours, just like we do with academic skills.

A truism to keep in mind is, "We get more of what we attend to":

> If we attend to disruptive behaviours, we will get more disruptive behaviours.

> If we attend to positive behaviours, we will get more positive behaviours.

Positive Reinforcement in Action

View the Movie to see an example of positive reinforcement in action. Yes, the effects are somewhat exaggerated for the sake of the sitcom. No, we don't want to reinforce students with candy every time. But the point is clear - positive behaviours increase when we reinforce and acknowledge them.

Movie 7.2 Positive Reinforcement - The Big Bang Theory
See the full video clip online http://youtu.be/JA96Fba-WHk

Address Reinforcement Myths

Five Reinforcement Myths to Bust!

There are five common myths about reinforcement that many people still believe. Share the truth with your staff and school community.

Reinforce positive behaviours

Reward people

Bust these dangerous myths:
1. Reinforcement and rewards are the same
2. Reinforcing students spoils them
3. Reinforcing students is bribery
4. Reinforcing students reduces intrinsic motivation
5. Reinforcement costs too much time and money

1. Reinforcement and Rewards are NOT the Same
Reinforcement is earned - like grades, a pay cheque, or a compliment. Rewards are not earned - people often get rewarded whether they earn it or not. Consider the bank executive who gets a bonus even during an economic recession or the wealthy student who receives a new phone or car for their birthday.

2. Reinforcing Students Does NOT Spoil Them
We regularly reinforce academic behaviours. Is it spoiling students when we give them an A+ they have earned? No, we simply call it feedback.

Think of reinforcement as feedback—it's OK to let students know when they are behaving correctly; it actually increases the chances of them doing it correctly again!

3. Reinforcing Students is NOT Bribery
Reinforcement is only bribery if used haphazardly to coerce students. Telling students they can receive 5 tickets for picking up trash is coercion and bribery - this is not appropriate. Coercion, like punishment, is not effective in the long run.

A reinforcement system is not coercion; it is a planned acknowledgment of specific desired behaviours. Specifically, the Expectations and Skills listed on your posters in each school location!

4. Reinforcing Students does NOT Reduce Intrinsic Motivation
Research evidence continually shows that positive reinforcement maintains intrinsic motivation for those that have it, and increases intrinsic motivation for those that don't.

Students who are already intrinsically motivated to behave do not stop when reinforcement is introduced into their environment. But reinforcement will help those who are not intrinsically motivated yet.

5. Reinforcements Does NOT Cost Too Much Time or Money
Too much time? How much time is currently wasted dealing with inappropriate behaviour and classroom disruptions? If we refocus our attention on appropriate behaviours we will have more positive behaviours and less inappropriate ones.

Too much money? There are hundreds of inexpensive ways to acknowledge and reinforce students for appropriate behaviour and many are free.

We recommend the ebook *Having Fun with PBIS: Free or No-cost Reinforcers for Appropriate Behavior* by Dr. Laura Riffel (behaviordoctorpublications.com) filled with over 76 pages of ideas and examples from schools.

> *In terms of the overall effects of reward, our meta-analysis indicates no evidence for detrimental effects of reward on measures of intrinsic motivation.*
> — Cameron, Banko & Pierce, 2001, p.21

Reinforcement = Relationships and Rapport

It is never a prize/reward that 'makes students behave'.

It is always the interaction and acknowledgment from a caring adult that reinforces and maintains positive social behaviours! By reinforcing students, we build relationships and rapport that we can rely on when there are difficult conversations or when we need to hold students accountable for their actions.

Reflection

Take a minute to anticipate being confronted with one of the reinforcement myths.

Using the reinforcement facts presented, how would you respond?

Create a Four Part Reinforcement Matrix

Many people equate reinforcement tickets with PBS. But that is only one part of the practices that make this system effective. Tickets are not effective in isolation! What makes PBS so effective is implementing a complete system.

Four Part Reinforcement System

1. Frequent Reinforcement
Something tangible (usually a ticket or coupon) given to students immediately upon demonstrating a specific skill from your Expectation Matrix.

2. Intermediate Reinforcement
A weekly or monthly drawing/raffle from frequent tickets for an item, activity or privilege that is reinforcing to students. We encourage schools to create a Reinforcement Menu of several items that students can choose from.

3. Long Term Reinforcement
A quarterly or semester drawing/raffle from frequent tickets for an item, activity or privilege that is reinforcing to students.

4. Staff Reinforcement
When students tickets are drawn, the staff who reinforced the student should be recognised - verbally or with an item, activity or privilege that is reinforcing to staff.

In a Reinforcement Matrix (Interactive 7.1), list When students will receive each type of reinforcement and What they will receive.

Interactive 7.1 Reinforcement Matrix Example

Reinforcement	When	What
Frequent	• When student is observed demonstrating a PBIS expectation/rule they receive a Ticket from staff • Ticket lists expectation plus student and staff names • Take ticket to office before/after class to redeem prize and 'Paw' • Ticket placed in PBIS box	• Tickets are carried by all staff • Prize is a pen/pencil from office (immediate) and student name on a 'Paw' posted in the main school hallway (end of day)
Intermediate	• Principal draws 20 names from PBIS Box every Friday at 2 PM • Students pick up prizes from office at 3 PM	• Certificate to take home • Photo on PBIS bulletin board
	• Principal draws 10 names from PBIS Box on the 1st of each month	• VISA (Very Important Student Access) pass for following month
Long Term	• Principal draws 5 names from PBIS Box at end of semester assembly • Students given prize in front of school	• Donated prizes sponsored by parent teacher organization or community • Gift certificates, books, school branded clothes, other merchandise
Staff	• @ all drawings, when student is recognized, the referring teacher is also recognized	• Free lunch @ weekly draw • Preferred parking @ monthly draw • Gift card @ semester assembly

Frequent Reinforcement Ticket

The most common reinforcement acknowledgment is a ticket or coupon. Electronic reinforcement systems (pros and cons) are addressed in the next section. The same reinforcement system should apply whether schools use paper or electronic reinforcement.

Students should receive a ticket and verbal reinforcement from staff when they demonstrate one of the skills or rules on a school's Expectation Matrix. The reinforcement ticket can then be used to access intermediate and long term reinforcement opportunities.

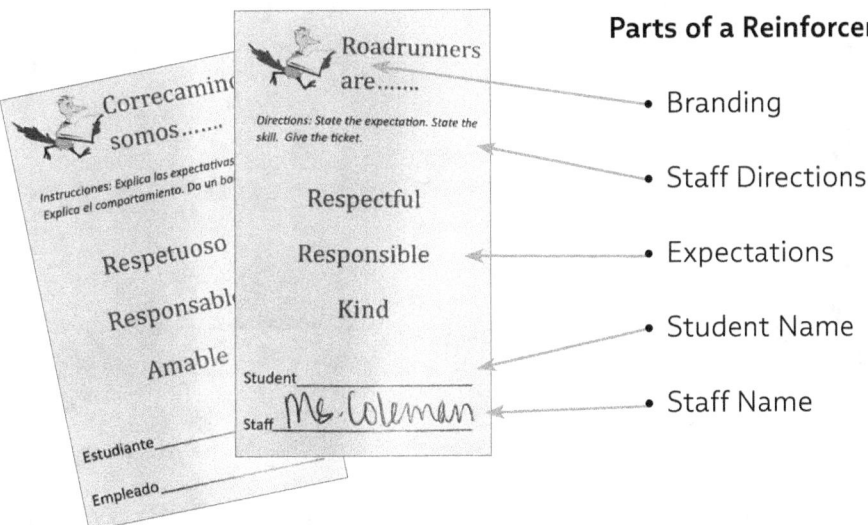

Parts of a Reinforcement Ticket:

- Branding
- Staff Directions
- Expectations
- Student Name
- Staff Name

3-Second/3-Step Reinforcement System

Review and share the Movie at the beginning of this chapter to see the system in action!

1. State the Expectation:
"Thank you for being Respectful..."

2. State the Skill:
"...by raising your hand and waiting to be called on."

3. Give the Ticket!

Rule of Thumb

1. Every student in school should receive at least 2 tickets/week.
2. If each staff member hands out 10 tickets per day (2 per hour), your school will easily meet this goal for the week.
3. This only adds up if ALL staff use tickets regularly!

These three steps seem simple but require practice. Give staff ample time to practice using these words and phrases.

See Gallery for examples of Frequent, Intermediate, Long term and Staff Reinforcement ideas.

Gallery 7.1

 Gallery 7.2

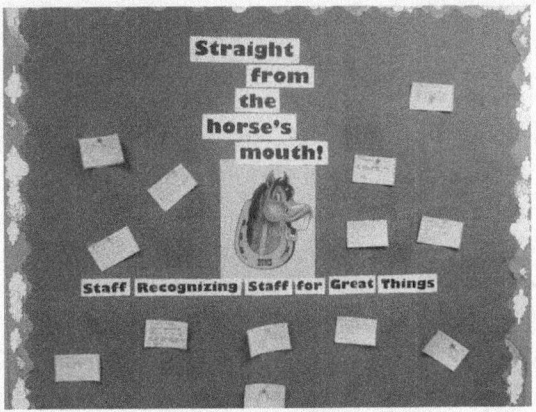

Reinforcement System

Frequent Electronic Reinforcement

Many schools have moved in to the 21st Century and are using electronic reinforcement practices. Some tools include PBISRewards and Hero or apps such as Class Dojo for younger students or Classcraft for older students. It's fine to reinforce electronically as long as you define your system in your Reinforcement Matrix.

Reminders:
- Align electronic points or tokens with your expectations and skills for each location in school. Students should earn points for the skills/rules listed on your posters - not for different behaviours.
- Use 3-Second/3-Step practices for delivering reinforcement every time.
- Consider how on-line points convert to on-ground intermediate and long-term drawings or recognition.
- NEVER take away tickets, points or tokens. Students quickly develop the view that it's pointless to earn tickets that can be taken away at any time - so why try.

Intermediate/Long-term Reinforcement

In the Reinforcement Matrix, we use a ticket drawing as an example of how to add intermittent and long-term practices to make a complete the reinforcement system.
But some schools are fond of using a Store to allow students to use their tickets to 'buy' reinforcement items. Please consider these pros and cons of running a school PBS Store.

School PBS Store	
Pros	**Cons**
- Tickets = $ - Tickets = choices - Charge more for high demand items - Charge less for low demand items or items you want to encourage students to purchase	- Tickets = $ - Store requires money to buy items. Where does the money come from, is it sustainable? - Store requires time to run and restock items. Who has the time, is it sustainable? - Store requires time for students to shop and make purchases. Are students missing teaching/learning/lunch/recess to visit the store? - $ can be lost or stolen. What is the school replacement policy, theft policy, bullying/harassment policy? - $ can be counterfeit. What is the school forgery policy? - $ can be used for coercion. What is the school bribery policy?

Other Cons to consider are the perception that a school store and monetary value given to tickets may have on your PBS System:

A monetary system:
- Gives a false perception that PBS is about prizes
- Gives a false perception that PBS is about extrinsic rewards
- Gives a false perception that the school is paying students to behave

Finally, school will have to contend with the fact that students who always behave will earn less money/tickets, and students who frequently misbehave will earn more money/tickets because they need more frequent reinforcement. By using a drawing/raffle system rather then a store, many of these Cons can be avoided.

Teach the Reinforcement System to Staff and Students

Create lesson plans and a system for teaching the Who, What, When, Where, Why of your Reinforcement Matrix for both staff and students.

The reinforcement system must be directly taught to teachers and staff and they need multiple opportunities to practice demonstrating the 3-Second/3-Step Reinforcement System.

Reflection

Take a minute to reflect on the two reinforcement videos.
What elements did you like from the two videos?
Could this approach work for your school - why or why not?

Advanced Reinforcement Strategies

Advanced strategies can be deployed after your Reinforcement Matrix and Tier 1 system is up and running.

Choose a strategy based on your behaviour data (Office Discipline Referrals) which will indicate where there is a need for additional supervision and monitoring of students.

Four Categories of Advanced Reinforcement Strategies with Endless Variations

1. Group Contingency by school, grade or department:
Reinforcement for the 'group' is 'contingent' upon meeting a goal.
- Challenge students to reduce ODR by a certain percent this week or month
- Contest to reduce Tardiness by 20% this week
- Contest to reduce class disruptions by 30% for the month of February
- Contest to reduce violations in the bathroom to ZERO for the next 10 days

2. Group Contingency by class or homeroom:
Reinforcement for the 'group' is 'contingent' upon meeting the goal.
- Each time the whole class demonstrates Respect (for example) a marble/ball/pencil is dropped in a jar
- Each time the whole class completes homework (a skill under Responsibility, for example) a marble/ball/pencil is dropped in a jar
- When the jar is full, class earns a reward

3. Criterion Based by Individual Student:
Everyone who meets the stated criteria receives the reinforcement.
- Students can earn extra reinforcement or privileges for zero ODR or Tardies or

Absences over a quarter
- These students receive a VISA Card = Very Important Student Access
- VISA includes 1/2 price events, 2 min. early release for lunch, 1 homework pass, 20% discount at school store

4. Targeted Blitz by Expectation and/or Location

Everyone who meets the criteria by demonstrating the targeted Expectation in the specified location at the moment the blitz is announced receives reinforcement.

- For example: a fire drill or hall sweep - announce a Blitz or Freeze for a particular expectation
- Every student demonstrating Responsibility with a proper dress code (for example) gets a ticket right now
- Every student demonstrating Respect in the cafeteria at today's lunch by saying "please/thank you" and cleaning their area gets a ticket
- Every student not tardy (Responsible by being in class on time, for example) receives reinforcement

Reflection

Take a minute to reflect on reinforcement strategies.
What is your favourite reinforcement strategy - why?
How will you use that strategy in your school?

Action Plan

1. Create a Reinforcement Matrix - gather staff/student input on free/inexpensive reinforcement ideas
2. Teach staff the Reinforcement System
3. Teach students the Reinforcement System

Resources

- 3-second/3-step Reward and Reinforcement Video
- Reinforcement Matrix
- *Having Fun with PBIS: Free or No-cost Reinforcers for Appropriate Behavior* by Dr. Laura Riffel behaviordoctorpublications.com

Available from koi-education.com/resources.

Evaluation

1. The four types of reinforcement needed in a PBS System include all of the following except:
   a. Long Term
   b. Intermediate
   c. Staff
   d. Frequent
   e. Short Term

2. Identify which step comes first when reinforcing expected behaviour:
   a. State the Expectation
   b. State the skill
   c. Give the ticket

3. Teaching the Reinforcement System is optional:
   a. True
   b. False

Answers: 1e, 2a, 3b

Chapter 8
Accountability System

A CONSISTENT ACCOUNTABILITY OR DISCIPLINE SYSTEM IS ESSENTIAL TO CREATING AN EQUITABLE SCHOOL CLIMATE FOR ALL.

Accountability System

Learning Objectives

Establish Defined Behaviours

Create a Behaviour Flowchart

Develop Forms & Procedures

Use a Database System

 Movie 8.1 Accountability Introduction

Dr. Jannasch-Pennell uses a chilling example to explain why a consistent accountability or discipline system is essential to avoid Dirty Data! View at http://youtu.be/O5TozicP4mE

Preview

An accountability system creates consistency, provides a clear distinction between office managed and classroom managed behaviours, provides definitions for behaviours and identifies predictable discipline procedures and consequences.

With an accountability system, schools can look forward to having clean data and a more equitable school climate.

Four Parts of an Accountability System

1. Defined Behaviours
2. Behaviour Flowchart
3. Forms & Procedures
4. Database System

See the Accountability System graphic below.

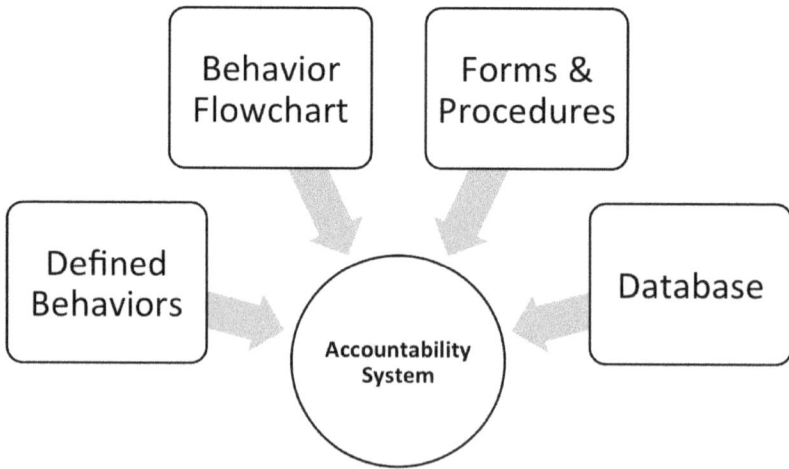

Establish Defined Behaviours

In many schools there are often inconsistent beliefs regarding which behaviours should be managed by staff versus behaviours which need to be managed by the office or school administrator. This inconsistency can lead to inequitable discipline - with some students, grades or ethnicities being disciplined more than others.

Ask Yourself:
- Do all staff agree on how behaviours are currently handled?
- Is there consistency in everyone's choices?
- Are clear definitions of what should be handled by staff and what should go to the office needed?

It is crucial to take time as a staff to discuss and create a list of minor behaviours vs. major behaviours, also known as staff managed behaviours vs. office managed behaviours.

The purpose of the T-Chart Activity is to help staff notice if there is a discrepancy between what everyone believes is a minor behaviour that should be managed by staff vs. major behaviours that should always be referred to the office. Often, the same behaviour is placed on both sides of the T-Chart indicating a discrepancy or inconsistency in the current accountability system.

The following activity can take a school staff between 20-60 minutes, depending on how close or far apart their current beliefs are. But, without a definitive list, some staff will continue to send some students to the office for what they consider major behaviour problems, while other staff will not write a referral for the exact same behaviour. That is the definition of inequity!

T-Chart Activity:

Material: T-Chart, Post-It Notes, markers and pens.

See Gallery for examples of the activity.

1. Ask each person to independently write down 3 minor behaviours and 3 major behaviours: one behaviour per sticky note.
2. Assign maximum 20 people per T-Chart.
3. Ask each person to place their sticky notes on the corresponding side of their assigned T-Chart.
4. After all notes are posted, Activity leader at each T-Chart will identify discrepancies - instances where the same behaviour was placed by some people on the major side and by some people on the minor side.

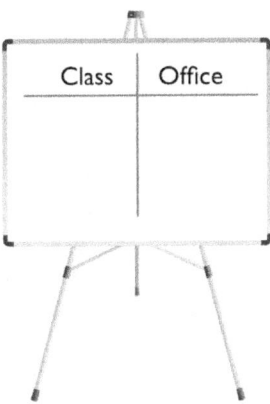

Discuss discrepancies and work toward consensus on listing each behaviour as either Minor or Major (this may take some time/debate).

*The office must manage and know about certain behaviours according to state/federal law or your school district policies.

 Gallery 8.1 Defined Behaviour Activity

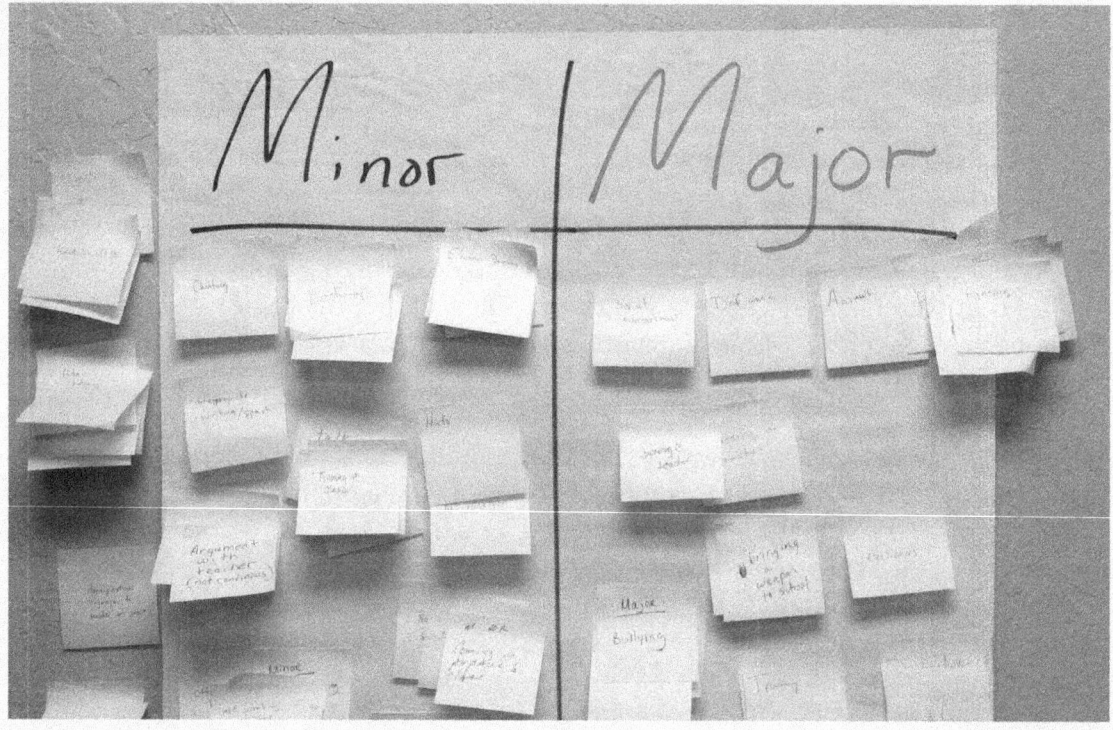

Minor (classroom) vs Major (office) T-Chart

Desert Mountain School, Deer Valley USD

Boulder Creek High School, Deer Valley USD

Reflection

*Take a minute to reflect on the T-Chart activity.
Why is it worth the time to do the T-Chart activity?
Why is doing this activity more relevant than simply telling staff that the current discipline practices are not consistent?*

Create a Behaviour Flowchart

What happens when a student disrupts the learning of others? Is discipline at your school:

- Consistent across all staff?
- Predictable across all staff?
- Equitable across all staff?

If discipline is not consistent, predictable or equitable, it's likely that both staff and students will feel frustrated and the climate at the school may not be very positive or welcoming.

To be consistent, schools need to develop common procedures for holding students accountable to the school-wide Expectations (created, taught, and reinforced in the last three chapters). All staff should be involved in creating these procedures to ensure buy-in and ownership from the people who are expected to hold students accountable. If procedures are too complicated, considered too time-consuming, or simply unmanageable, they will not be implemented consistently and schools are back to an inequitable discipline system.

The PBS tool schools use to create consistent student accountability is called a Behaviour Flowchart. The Behaviour Flowchart will become the procedures all staff will follow when they see minor or major behaviours - so be sure you can live with it and follow it. If not, keep discussing it! Remember, the reason for a Behaviour Flowchart is consistent, predictable, and equitable accountability to your school-wide Expectations.

Consider Movie 8.2 as a comical way to introduce common problems with an inequitable and inconsistent discipline system.

Movie 8.2 School Data - A Comedy
"We don't want no dirty data messing up our school." Retrieved from http://youtu.be/XBu95uMFudE

See the next section for Flowchart considerations, a Gallery of examples and an activity that allows staff to discuss and decide on consistent interventions for minor or staff managed behaviour problems.

Considerations for Creating a Behaviour Flowchart:

1. Align with School-Wide Expectations
If students are not Respectful, Responsible or Safe, what is going to be the consistent feedback/intervention from staff the first, second, or third time the same minor behaviour occurs? At what point is an ODR written?

2. Staff managed procedures
Redirect, remind or reteach expectations should be the first interventions. Accountability must be linked to Expectations.

3. Track and record interventions
Document minor behaviours and interventions - a quick checklist. See next section for rationale and Figure 8.1 for forms.

4. Include effective interventions at the classroom level
Examples may include: teacher proximity, re-direct, re-locate, a reflection sheet, or to review academic competency.

5. Office managed procedures
Repeated minor, and major behaviours, should result in an ODR. The consequence must align with school, policy not administrator whim. Always provide feedback to referring teacher/staff.

6. Plan lessons to teach staff and students the policies and procedures
Never assume the Flowchart is self-explanatory! See Teaching Accountability chapter for a Case Study lesson plan.

 **Gallery 8.2 Behaviour Flowchart Examples**

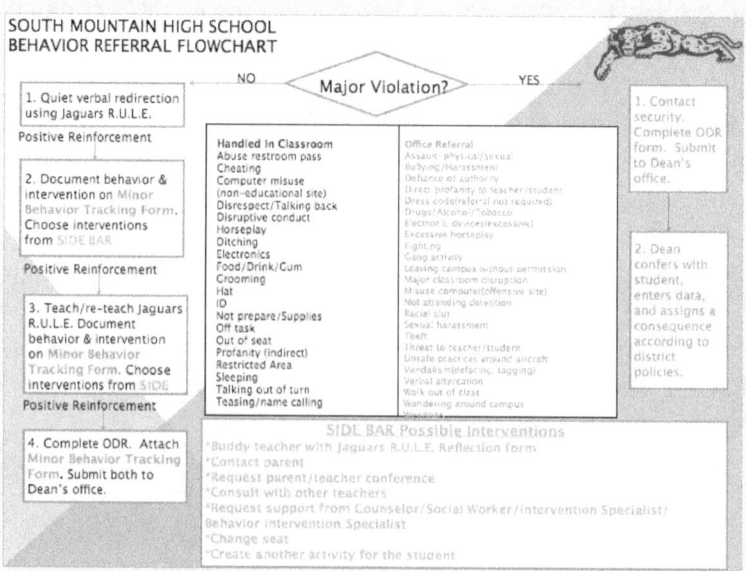

Gallery 8.2 Behaviour Flowchart Examples (continued)

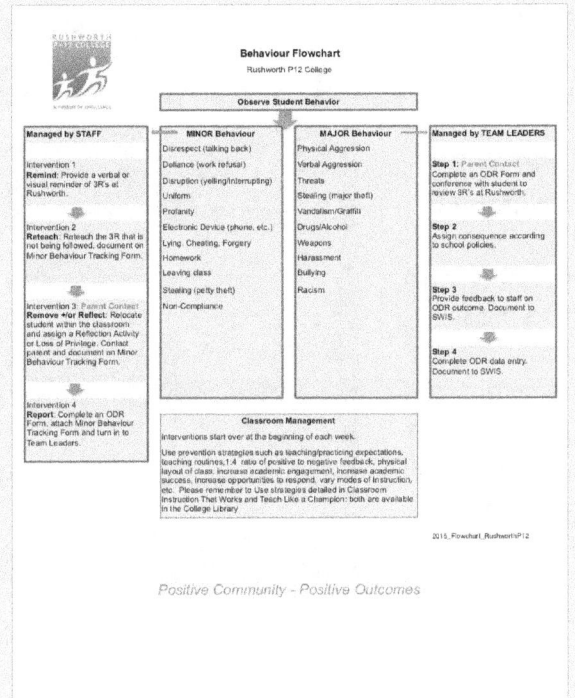
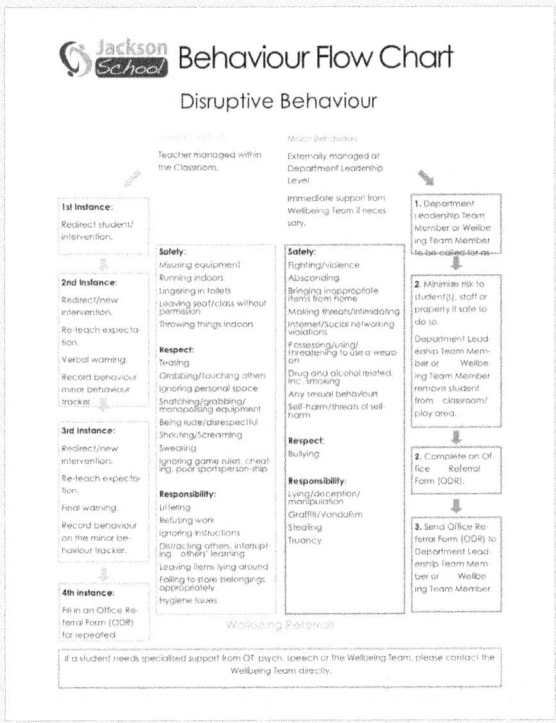
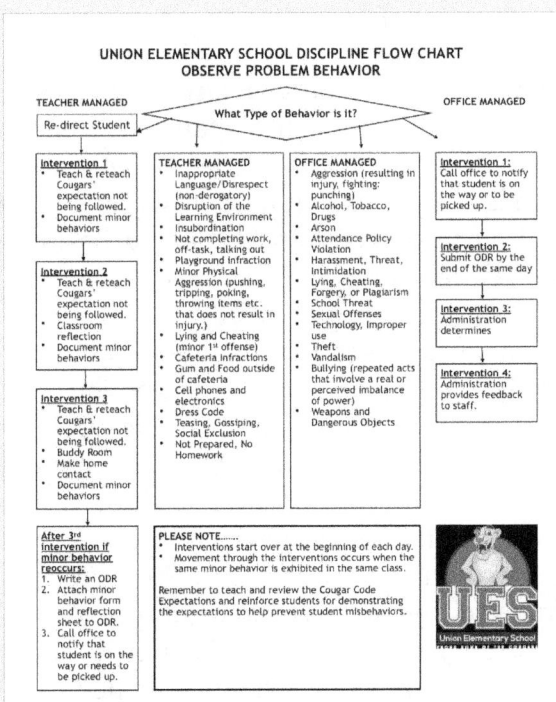
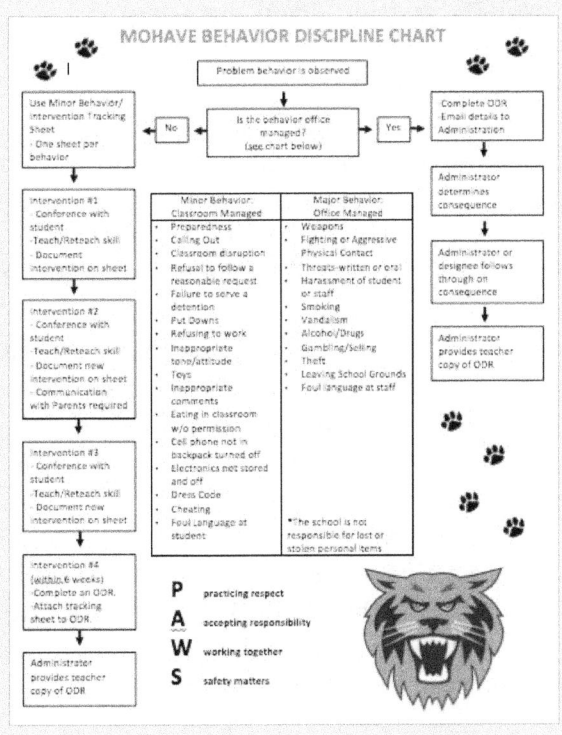

 **Movie 8.3 Referral Process and PBIS at Grijalva Elementary**

Take a moment to watch a teacher respond to minor classroom disruptions by following her school's Behaviour Flowchart interventions. Retrieved from https://youtu.be/fgSH6seZD2s

Behaviour Flowchart Activity, Minor Interventions:

Material: Chart paper, Post-It Notes, markers and pens.

1. Ask staff to brainstorm interventions for minor behaviours (in the classroom, cafeteria, playground, hall, etc.)
2. List interventions on chart paper (as they are called out)
3. Discuss the list, and rank in order of least to most intrusive consequence.
4. Decide when a repeated minor behaviour is recorded as an Office Discipline Referral (ODR). On the example in the picture, the staff decided on three interventions. Your staff need to decide how many times they want to intervene with the same repeated minor behaviour before the student is written up and sent to the office?

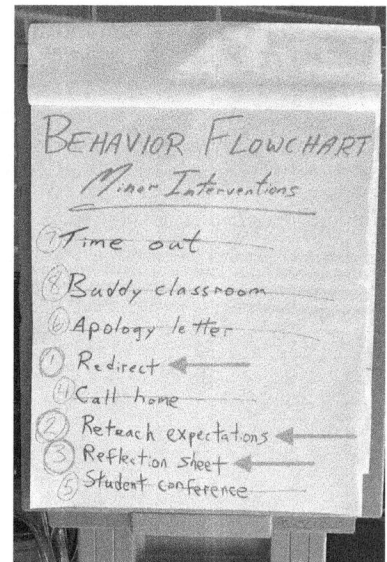

Develop Forms and Procedures

Minor Behaviour Tracking Form

The purpose of a Minor Behaviour Tracking Form is not to require extra paperwork. It is just a checklist to track interventions listed on the Behaviour Flowchart and help staff consistently hold students accountable for their minor behaviours before an ODR is written (if necessary). It can also be used to identify students with frequent misbehaviours that never result in an ODR but who are in need of additional behaviour supports. Each intervention for minor behaviours on the Flowchart should remind staff to document the intervention.

For example, physical education or music teachers might only see a student once a week, whereas high school teachers may see 120+ students per day - how can they possibly remember which interventions they've implemented with a particular student this week or this month? Relying on memory alone is sure to lead to biased or inequitable accountability.

- Decide if minor interventions reset to a 'clean slate' on a weekly or monthly basis (restarting feedback at Intervention #1 for a repeated minor behaviour). This will determine the Minor Behaviour Tracking Form used (see examples in Figure).
- If a student only receives an intervention in September, December and March it means that the Flowchart is working - not three strikes and you are out! If students need interventions daily, it means the Flowchart is not working for them and they need additional Tier 2 or Tier 3 support.

- A weekly 'clean slate' will lead to less office referrals (less data) because a student has multiple chances to correct their behaviour every week before receiving an ODR for their minor behaviour. This works well for younger students who need extra practice and corrective feedback...and are less likely to remember that they received an intervention 3 weeks ago!
- A monthly 'clean slate' will lead to more office referrals (more data) because the student receives fewer chances to correct their behaviour each month before receiving an ODR. We expect older students to remember feedback and meet expectations that have been taught and retaught.
- Minor Behaviours Tracking Forms DO NOT follow the student from class to class to 'catch them being bad'. Every staff is responsible for tracking the interventions they have delivered to a student. If a student receives an ODR for being disruptive in math, in the cafeteria, and in the hall by three different staff, these three ODRs tell the PBS team that this student needs more support and different interventions for this particular behaviour. ODR = key to support.

Common Misperceptions

If a student, Jane, is disruptive, then disrespectful, and then later in the week or month she is defiant regarding an assignment, this does not mean that Jane should receive three successive interventions from the Behaviour Flowchart and is due for an ODR. Each of these behaviours is different and each should result in the first intervention on your Behaviour Flowchart only (which is why tracking is necessary).

Note that in the example above, Jane wasn't disruptive again, or disrespectful again or defiant again - the Flowchart accountability worked! If Jane received an ODR, this would be the academic equivalent of providing corrective feedback when she misspelt a word, then miscalculated a number, and later forgot to use punctuation or capitalisation in writing - and the teacher saying, "This is the third time I've corrected you, go to the office!". Providing corrective feedback once for three different academic behaviours is the same as providing corrective feedback once for three different social behaviours. The Minor Behaviour Tracking Form helps us track our feedback so that accountability is consistent, predictable and equitable for all students. See the Teaching Accountability Chapter for a Case Study example to teach your Accountability System.

Figure 8.1 Minor Tracking Forms

ODR Referral Form

Staff need to understand why Office Discipline Referral (ODR) forms are important. The purpose of ODRs is to identify and get support to students with behaviour problems. If staff do not write ODRs for repeated minor behaviours or for a major behaviour, that means there is no problem. No problems means no solution or support for the student. That doesn't help anyone! We need to see ODRs as keys to support - not a tool for punishment or shame.

Do all staff fill out your Office Discipline Referral (ODR) form correctly, completely and consistently? If not, you may have Dirty Data.

ODR forms need to collect the following information (we'll show how to analyse/use this data in the Data Analysis Chapter):

ODR Checklist	
✔ Student Name	✔ Problem Behaviour (minor or major)
✔ Grade	✔ Perceived Motivation
✔ Referring Staff	✔ Others Involved
✔ Date of Incident	✔ Action Taken by Administrator
✔ Time of Incident	✔ Seclusion/Restraint
✔ Location of Incident	• All items, except Seclusion/Restraint, are required by the SET Evaluation

The order of the items in your ODR form should mimic the order they appear in your electronic database entry page. This makes it more efficient to enter data.

Electronic ODR forms must be accessible to ALL staff since problem behaviours often occur outside of the classroom. Consider how recess or cafeteria staff, substitute/temporary teachers, security guards or crossing guards will report and record problem behaviours. Remember: no ODR = no problem = no solution!

ODR Paper Handling Procedures

As a team, develop procedures so there is consistency and a systematic way to manage ODRs at your school.

Here are some questions to discuss when developing your paper handling procedures.
- Who, when, and how will staff be trained on using the ODR form?
- Once written, where does ODR go?
- Who decides on the official violation?
- Where does ODR go until entered into the system?
- When and who enters the data?
- When and who gets reports, analyses, and shares data with staff?

Write up, teach, then distribute ODR procedures to staff (via a staff handbook, for example) to ensure clean data for decision-making.

Use a Database System

Key Features of Data Systems that Work

It is essential that behaviour and discipline data is entered into a computerised database.

- Data needs to be accurate and valid
- Data must be easy to collect, it should only take about 1% of staff time
- Data needs to be automatically presented as graphs

Furthermore, data must be used for decision-making. Therefore, data must be accessible and available when decisions need to be made. Teachers must be shown that the data in ODR's is used to make decisions.

Taking into account these key features of data systems that work, let's explore two types of database systems:

Student Information Systems (SIS)
Most schools have some type of student information or student management software to enter academic, attendance and/or discipline data. The potential problem is that many databases only collect data and it is challenging and time consuming to export and analyse data - especially in graphic form - to share with school staff and make decisions.

Talk to your Information Technology director to ask if your system can export the Big 7 Data graphs listed next.

School Wide Information System (SWIS)
SWIS is a web-based information system that collects, tracks and provides graphical reports easily and efficiently at the press of a button. It provides the 'Big 7' PBS data graphs and the ability to 'drill down' and filter data graphs to answer many different questions about student behaviour. This database is used by over 25,000 PBS schools across the nation, Europe and Australia. It was developed and is managed by the University of Oregon as part of a federal education grant. See a SWIS demo at PBISapps.org.

See the Data Analysis Chapter for a checklist of graphs and reports that are required from your database system.

'Big 7' Data Graphs

PBS teams rely on seven graphs created from the data entered into the ODR forms to identify where PBS is working effectively on a school campus and where it is not. These 'Big 7' graphs can also show teams which students PBS is working for and which students need more support. This information enables PBS teams to identify and solve problems quickly and efficiently.

See an example of graphs in the next Gallery.

The *KOI PBS Tier 2 Manual* includes deeper insights into using ODR data to identify students who need support, match their specific behaviour with targeted Tier 2 programs, and teaches several of the most common programs to decrease behaviour problems in school and refocus on teaching and learning.

Big 7 Graphs	
1. Average Referrals	• Average incidents per day per month
2. Problem Behaviours	• Frequency of different behaviours
3. Students	• Frequency of incidents per student
4. Grade Level	• Frequency of incidents per grade
5. Location	• Frequency of incidents per location
6. Time of Day	• Frequency of incidents by time
7. Day of Week	• Frequency of incidents each day

Reflection

Take a minute to reflect on the database graphs.
Can your database graph ODR data?
Can it create graphs with one or two 'clicks'?
If not (to either question), what will you do about it?

Gallery 8.3 'Big 7' Data Graphs
SWIS Dashboard from PBISapps.org. Tap any graph to customise or drill down to get answers quickly and easily.

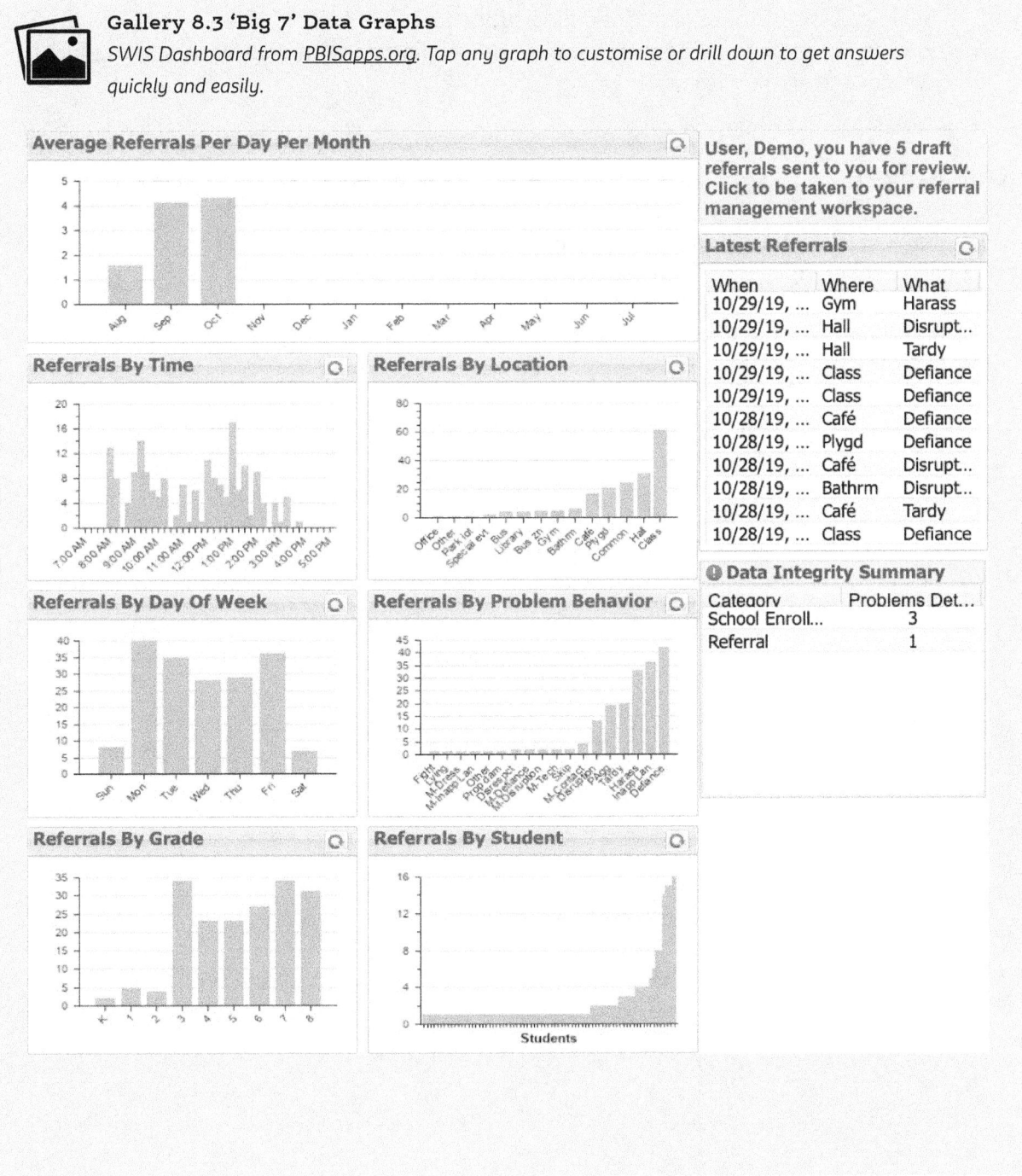

Action Plan

1. Define Behaviours: Use a T-Chart activity to identify classroom managed (minor) vs. office managed (major) behaviours
2. Define Minor/Major Interventions: Follow activity to create a Behaviour Flowchart with staff input
3. Review/Revise/Create an Office Discipline Referral (ODR) Form
4. Choose a Minor Behaviour Tracking Form that aligns with your Flowchart
5. Review/Revise/Create paper handling procedures
6. Identify a database system that collects discipline data and easily prints graphs of the data to share with staff

Resources

- Behaviour Flowchart (Template) and Examples
- ODR Form Template
- ODR Paper Handling Procedures
- Minor Behaviour Tracking Form
- SIS-DAD Checklist

Available from koi-education.com/resources.

Evaluation

1. Why is there a need to differentiate between minor vs. major behaviours?
   a. Consistency
   b. Equity
   c. Clean data
   d. All of the above

2. Every school needs to have a Behaviour Flowchart
   a. True
   b. False

3. Which item is not one of the "Big 7"
   a. Student
   b. Location
   c. Consequence
   d. Problem Behaviour
   e. Time of Day

4. Teaching the Accountability System is optional?
   a. True
   b. False

Answers: 1d, 2a, 3c, 4b

THIS PAGE INTENTIONALLY LEFT BLANK

Chapter 9
Teaching Accountability

SCHOOLS PRACTICE FIRE DRILL PROCEDURES REGULARLY.

HOW OFTEN DO WE PRACTICE MANAGING CLASSROOM BEHAVIOUR?

Teaching Accountability

Learning Objectives
Display the Behaviour Flowchart
Create Lesson Plans and a Case Study
Schedule Training for Staff and Students

School Safety is an Important and Serious Topic

Most schools have emergency procedures in case of fire, evacuation or lock-down on campus. These plans are required (by state or local jurisdiction) to be taught and practised with staff and students multiple times per year to ensure that they are implemented correctly. Even though a fire, evacuation or lock-down is not a regular occurrence schools, staff can recite the multi-step procedures involved in these drills with consistency and precision.

Classroom disruptions are much more common than emergency events. Yet, too often staff cannot recall the process for addressing behaviour problems at their school. Let's give the same amount of attention to teach and practice the process for addressing behaviour problems (the Behaviour Flowchart, ODR Form and Minor Behaviour Tracking Form) that we give to emergency plans.

This chapter will help schools create a teaching system to assure that all staff know the accountability system in place at their school.

Preview

In previous chapters, we discussed the importance of teaching the Expectation and Reinforcement Systems. It is also critical to teach the four parts of the Accountability System. We recommend following the same objectives listed in the Teaching System Chapter:

1. Display the expectation (Behaviour Flowchart)
2. Create lesson plans (a Case Study)
3. Schedule training for staff and students

Display the Behaviour Flowchart

The Behaviour Flowchart is your tool for ensuring that students are held accountable to your expectations consistently and equitably. It also helps schools identify which students need additional tiers of behaviour support. As such, it should be displayed in all areas where you post expectations:

- Classroom and learning areas
- Hallways/walkways and common areas
- Offices and cafeteria
- School bus

As with posting expectations: make a list of locations, print posters large enough to read from across the room, and print extra in case some are removed accidentally.

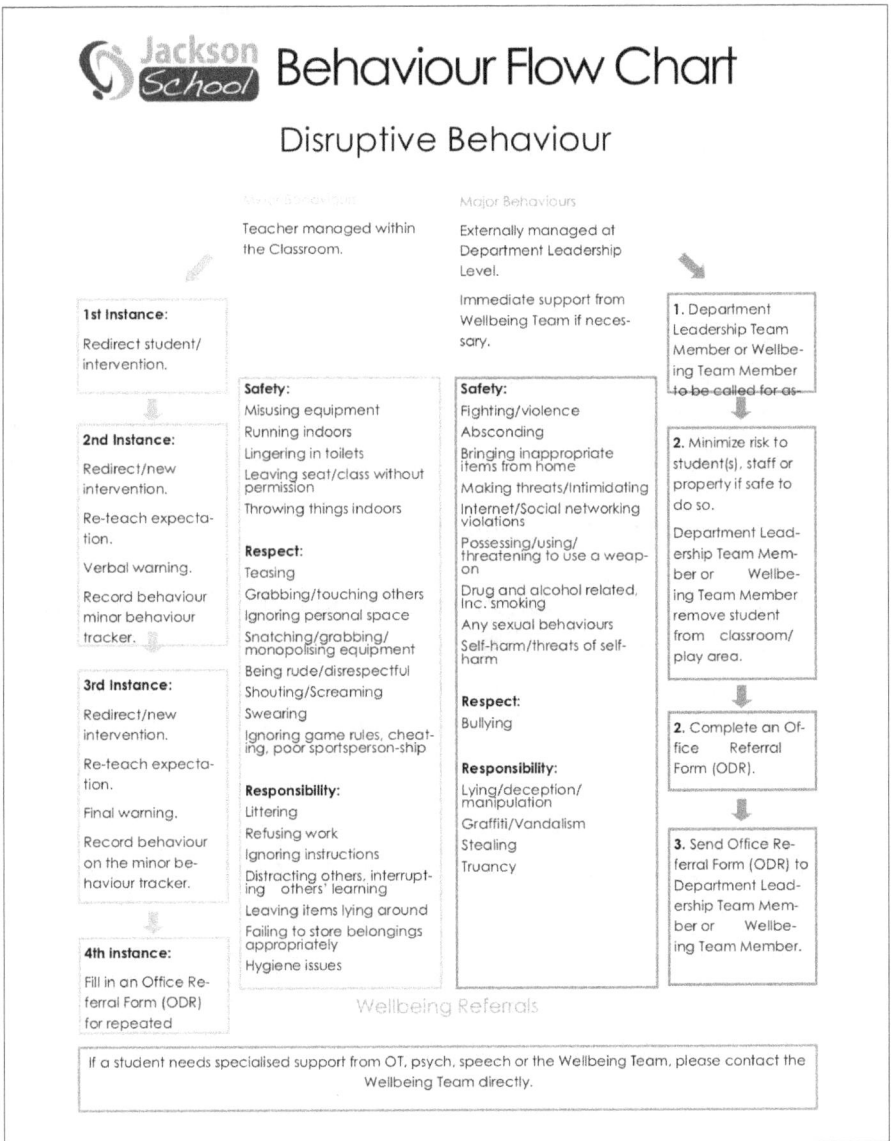

Create Lesson Plans and a Case Study

Two components of the Accountability System need to be taught and practised:

- Behaviour Flowchart (staff and students)
- ODR form and procedures (staff)

Staff may ask, "Why should we teach the Behaviour Flowchart and to students?". Possible answers are:

"We want to teach students the flowchart so they know what to expect if they do not meet and follow school-wide Expectations."

"Teaching students the referral process will not encourage students to 'manipulate' or 'cheat' the system. Those students who are always pushing boundaries may be signalling that they need additional tiers of behaviour support."

Students
Lesson plans for teaching students the Behaviour Flowchart can use the same lesson plan template introduced in the Teaching System Chapter.

Staff
Staff need multiple opportunities to practice applying the Behaviour Flowchart and completing the ODR and Minor Behaviour Tracking Form (MBTF). A Case Study approach allows staff to practice using the Flowchart with several different behaviour scenarios. Throughout the year, the Case Study can be adapted and differentiated to reteach parts of your accountability system that staff struggle completing correctly or consistently.

Case Study to Teach the Behaviour Flowchart

Download the Case Study slide presentation from koi-education.com/resources, and customise using your schools' Behaviour Flowchart.

Four cases or behaviour scenarios are available. The first case is simple and introduces only one repeated minor behaviour requiring staff to intervene and follow the Behaviour Flowchart procedures.

The cases get progressively more complex, much like a typical day in school.

Case Study #1: On Monday, Johnny is off-task during a math lesson. Twenty minutes later he is off-task again searching through his backpack. Wednesday, he is off-task while he is supposed to be working in a group. Later on that period, he is off-task while he is supposed to be doing independent reading. Friday, he is off-task talking to his friends.

Directions: Discuss in small groups. According to our Behaviour Flowchart:

1. Decide if this is a minor or major behaviour.
2. Discuss what staff should do first, second, third, etc.

Goal: For all staff reach consensus on point #1 and #2. When there is disagreement, discuss until an agreement is reached on how to follow the Flowchart in this case.

A Case Study approach allows staff to hold 'courageous conversations' about managing problem behaviours consistently and predictably so that when a student does X, all staff will do Y. After building rapport with students, it is consistency in accountability that leads to positive changes student behaviour.

Consistent application of the accountability system is important so that:
- there is equity in discipline across staff and students, (regardless of race, ethnicity, gender, socio-economic status or academic achievement)
- behaviour data is clean, reliable and can be used for solving student problems
- behaviour problems decrease resulting in more time for teaching and learning

PBS Team Tip:
If staff are consistently interpreting the Behaviour Flowchart differently, then the PBS team may need to re-draft the Flowchart to clear up ambiguity and re-teach the Case Studies again.

One way to reduce ambiguity and misunderstanding in the first place is to get staff buy-in and ownership when creating your Behaviour Flowchart using the activities suggested in the Accountability System Chapter and methods listed in the Ownership Systems Chapter.

Lesson Plans to Teach the ODR Forms and Procedures

Never assume that forms are easy to use and straight forward to fill out. Always confirm and assess understanding, after teaching.

ODR and MBTF Form
Complete an ODR and MBTF for a minor behaviour with staff (during the Case Study activity), line by line, to ensure common understanding of each item on the form. Repeat for a major ODR. Call staff attention to these common ODR mistakes:

- Time - refers to the time of the incident, not the time staff wrote the referral.
- Problem Behaviour - should be the last (most serious) behaviour exhibited by the student that resulted in the ODR. This will ensure the database tracks the problem that receives a consequence. The ODR may be for fighting, even if there was profanity and defiance before the incident.
- All behaviour narratives must be objective: "Bill threw a pen at a peer". Not subjective: "Bill had a bad temper and was being snotty".
- Most school data is public record, make sure your ODR report doesn't make headlines in the local or national newspaper!

Office Procedures
Teach the Paper Handling Procedures Checklist developed as part of the Accountability System Chapter.

Schedule Training for Staff and Students

Refresh yourself on this objective in the Teaching Systems Chapter for an in-depth review of the '5 W Questions' you need to make decisions about:

Who
Who will teach the lessons and case study? PBS leadership team, administrators, department chairs, students?

What
Student lesson plans, staff Case Study, staff lesson plans for ODR, staff lesson plan for MBTF forms?

When
When will training occur? Before the school year begins, grade level team meetings, professional learning community time, in the first-period class?

Where
Where will training occur? Whole staff meeting, department meetings, small/large groups, classroom?

How
How will the training occur? A live lecture, slideshow, video modelling, online modules via a learning management system?

> ### Reflection
>
> *Take a minute to finish this sentence:*
> *Teaching our Accountability System will work great if...*

Action Plan

1. Print and post the Behaviour Flowchart in each school location where it is required.
2. Create a lesson plan to teach the Behaviour Flowchart to students.
3. Customise the Case Study presentation with your Behaviour Flowchart for the staff.
4. Create a lesson plan to teach the office procedures to staff.
5. Schedule training for staff and students.

Resources

- Case Study slides
- Lesson Plan template (see Teaching Systems Chapter)
- ODR Paper Handling Procedures

Available from koi-education.com/resources.

Evaluation

1. How are school safety (fire drill or lock-down) and the behaviour flowchart similar?
   a. Complex procedures
   b. OK to review once a year
   c. Common sense
   d. All of the above

2. Where should the Behaviour Flowchart be displayed?
   a. Classroom
   b. Hallways
   c. Office
   d. School bus
   e. All of the above

3. Why use a Case Study to teach staff the Behaviour Flowchart?
   a. Staff are slow
   b. Staff need practice with procedures
   c. Staff like talking about problems
   d. Staff can argue the merits of the flowchart

4. Schedule training for:
   a. All staff
   b. Teachers
   c. Administrators
   d. Parents

Answers: 1a, 2e, 3b, 4a

Chapter 10
Data Analysis

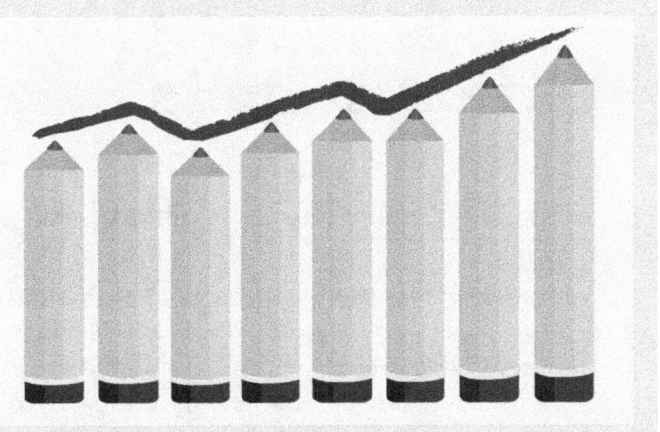

HOWEVER BEAUTIFUL YOUR STRATEGY YOU SHOULD OCCASIONALLY LOOK AT RESULTS.

— WINSTON CHURCHILL

Data Analysis

Learning Objectives

Understand Data Graphs

Analyse Monthly Data

Share Data Monthly

 Movie 10.1 Funny school video of kid taking a test

Without clean data, you don't know Jack! http://youtu.be/yPDOgpfKLuo

Preview

PBS is defined by three essential elements: Systems, Practices, and Data. Data is used to measure if PBS implementation is impacting outcomes or not (objectively, not subjectively). Having clean data is critical to assess which students need additional support to be successful.

This chapter will show you how to use data (collected with a 4-Part Accountability system) for decision-making and how to analyse behaviour data quickly and easily.

Understanding Data Graphs

Office Discipline Referral (ODR) data (all 10 items specified in the ODR Checklist in the Accountability System Chapter) should be entered into a computerised database daily. This will enable the school administrator to look up previous consequences for a student before deciding on a consequence for a new or continuing behaviour problem. Data, once entered, should be automatically graphed to allow the PBS team to quickly answer Who/What/When/Where are behaviour problems occurring at school - so they can solve the problems! Understanding different data graphs is the first step in the data analysis process.

Big 7 Data Graphs

Data should be viewed as bar graphs because it's easier to see patterns and trends in a graph compared to a table of numbers. A Dashboard with the Big 7 behaviour data reports should be available from your database without the hassle of exporting and creating graphs each and every time new data is entered.

Big 7 Graphs
• Average Referrals per month (ODR/days) • Students • Grade • Problem Behaviour • Time of Day • Day of Week • Location

PBIS Tier 1 Manual

See examples of the Big 7 graphs in Gallery 10.1.

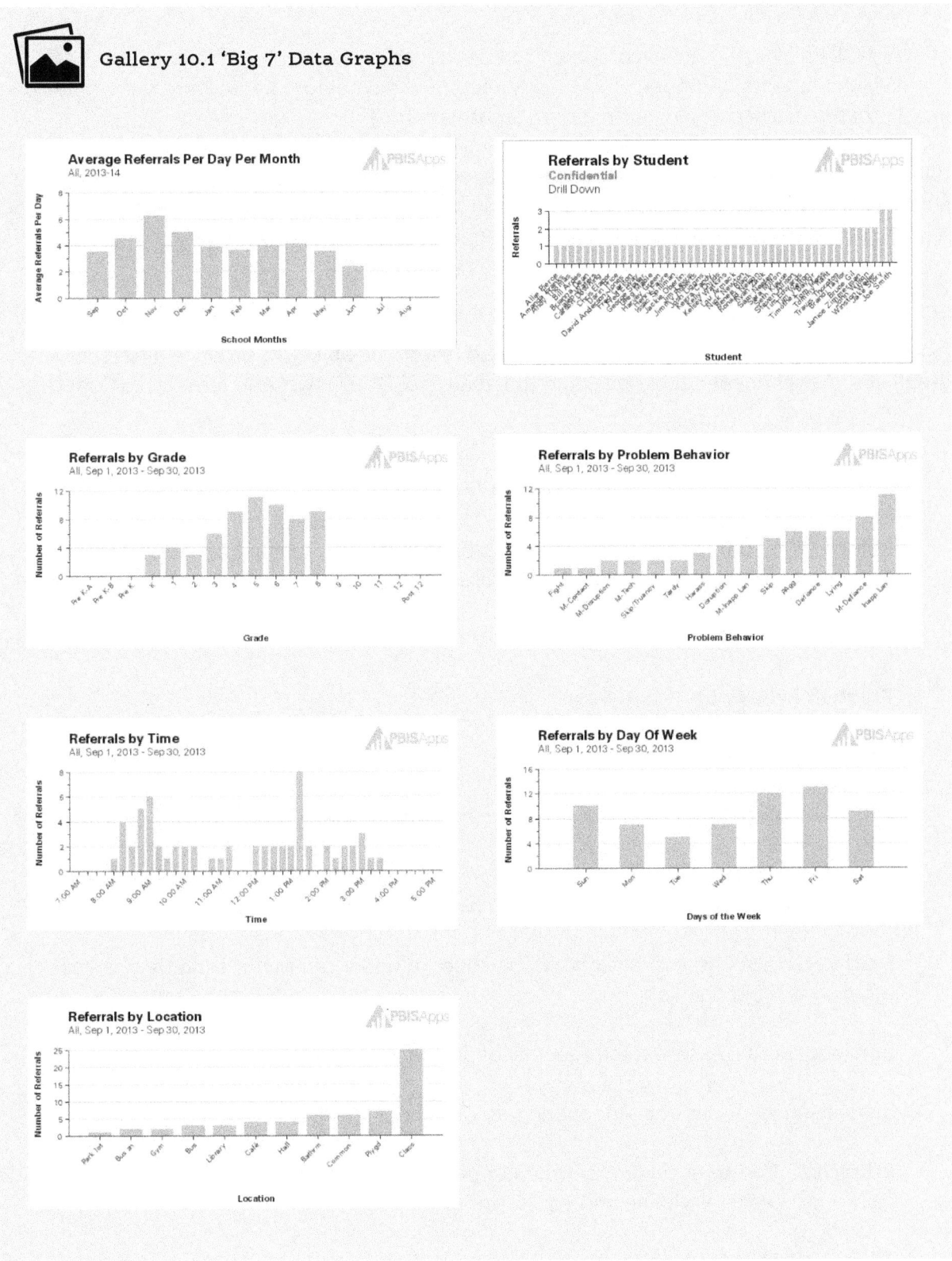

Gallery 10.1 'Big 7' Data Graphs

The Big 7 are the seven main graphs that PBS teams should be reviewing on a monthly basis to see the big picture of behaviour at a school. At a glance teams can answer:

- Are ODRs trending down compared to last month?
- Which students or grades or locations need help now before behaviours get worse?
- Is there a particular day or time that is problematic?

By focusing on reteaching or reinforcing the expectations that are not being followed in certain grades, locations or times, a school can prevent problems before they start. This allows staff more time and energy for teaching, learning and fun.

Additional Data Graphs

In addition to the Big 7 graphs, a database also needs the ability to produce different graphs to answer deeper questions, and the ability to 'Drill Down' and filter by each of the Big 7 categories.

Additional Data Graphs
- **Referral Rate per month** (ODR/students/days X 100) - Compare behaviour problems across schools within the district or across the country
- **Average Referrals** - Multi-year
- **Problem Behaviour** - Multi-year
- **Location** - Multi-year
- **Perceived Motivation** - Identify the function of behaviour
- **Non-IEP/IEP/504** - Compare referrals for students from different groups, such as students receiving special education services
- **Staff Referrals** - Assess which staff may over or under refer indicating they need more support or training
- **Consequences** - Assess the frequency of different consequences
- **Suspensions** - Assess in-school and out-of-school suspensions
- **Ethnicity** - Compare percent enrolled to percent referred to assess if disproportionate discipline and equity are problems
- **Triangle Data** - Assess behaviour support needed: Tier 1 = 0-1 ODRs, Tier 2 = 2-5 ODR, Tier 3 = 6+ ODRs

ODR & Data Analysis Connection

The Big 7 graphs and much of this additional data comes directly from the information entered into the ODR form. If the ODR form does not ask for this information or staff are not trained to complete the information correctly or all the data is not entered into the database in a timely fashion, then data analysis/decision-making/problem-solving is not possible. This is why the 4-Part Accountability System and Teaching the system are so important.

Counting ODR's

Data can be misleading. One school may report ODR Referral numbers to create their graph, another may use Average Referrals, and another may report their Referral Rate. What's the difference?

Referrals - Count every referral. This is helpful when comparing 2016 to 2017 to 2018. But some months have fewer days than others, so comparing September to December may be misleading. December should have fewer ODRs because there are fewer school days.

Average Referrals - ODR/days. This takes into account the number of days each month. Comparing September to December makes sense, but comparing one school to another (within the district or across the nation) is misleading. A school with fewer students should have fewer ODRs.

Referral Rate - ODR/students/days X 100. This takes into account the number of students in the school and the number of days in the month (or in the school year). It allows teams to compare their PBS system to another school in their district or other PBS schools across the nation.

Let's look at comparison graphs to illustrate the difference.

All graphs use the same number of ODRs (90) each month. Referral Rate lists the number of students at each school.

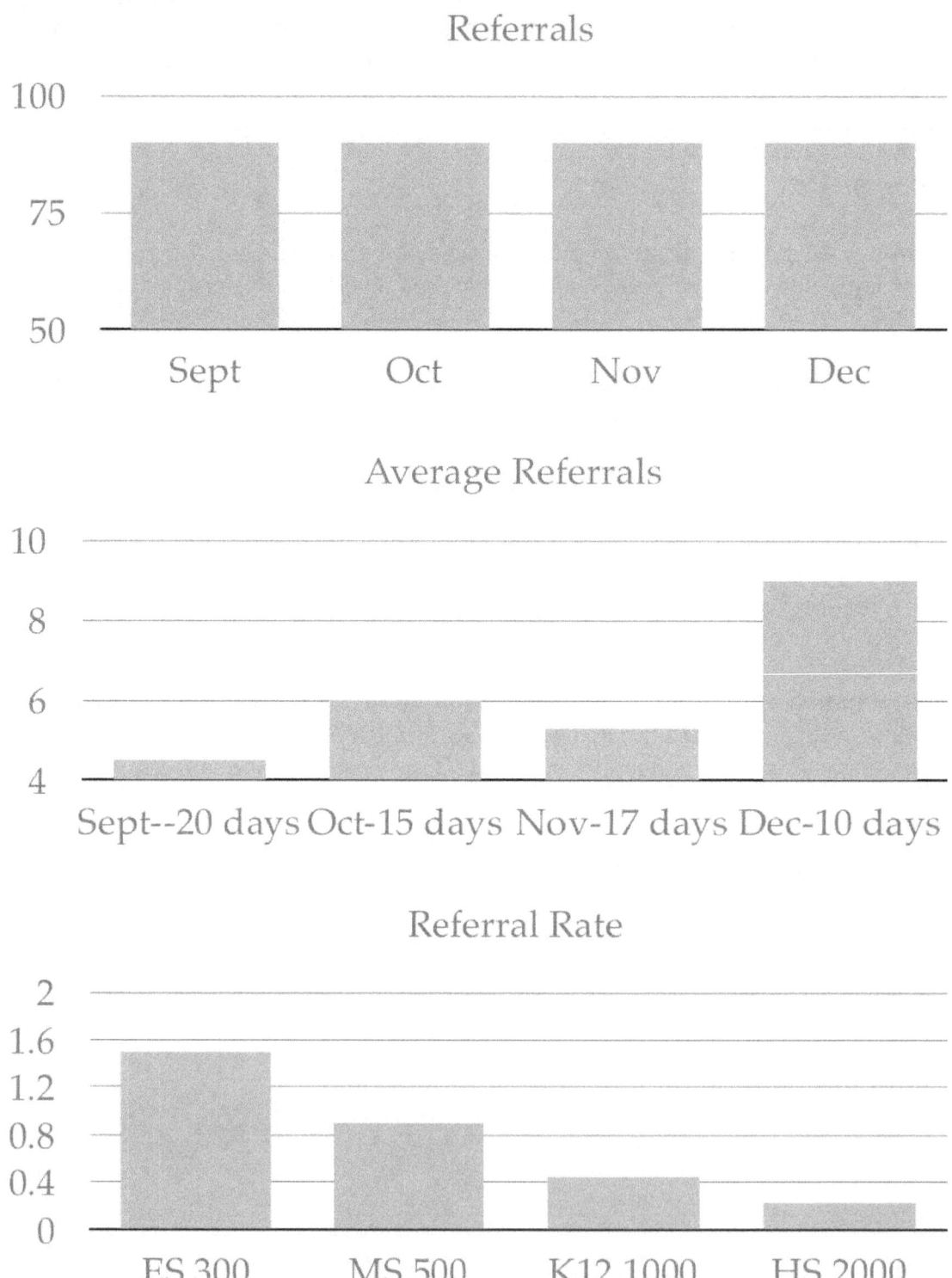

PBISapps.org publishes aggregated (anonymous) ODR data from across the nation so that schools can compare their Referral Rate to other PBS schools.

Figure 10.1 SWIS Comparison Table

SWIS Summary

2016–17 Academic Year
5716 Schools | 3,072,664 Students | 1,853,214 ODRs
Data Reported August 2017

MAJORS ONLY

Grade Range	Number of Schools	Mean Enrollment per School	Mean ODRs/100 Students/ School Day	Median ODRs/100 Students/ School Day	25th Percentile ODRs/100 Students/ School Day	75th Percentile ODRs/100 Students/ School Day
K-6	3582	469	.34 (.60)	.20	.09	.39
6-9	1024	643	.48 (.67)	.31	.15	.57
9-12	526	931	.48 (.71)	.28	.16	.53
PreK-8	363	427	.55 (1.84)	.27	.12	.51
PreK-12	92	308	.90 (2.15)	.26	.15	.65

ODR=office discipline referral; (#)=standard deviation; Shaded column=most useful for decision making

MINORS ONLY

Grade Range	Number of Schools	Mean Enrollment per School	Mean ODRs/100 Students/ School Day	Median ODRs/100 Students/ School Day	25th Percentile ODRs/100 Students/ School Day	75th Percentile ODRs/100 Students/ School Day
K-6	2952	461	.44 (.73)	.25	.10	.54
6-9	786	606	.57 (.73)	.35	.13	.72
9-12	380	885	.39 (.66)	.17	.06	.43
PreK-8	308	427	.73 (2.14)	.31	.11	.64
PreK-12	84	309	.72 (.72)	.41	.20	.98

ODR=office discipline referral; (#)=standard deviation; Shaded column=most useful for decision making

Culturally Responsive PBS Data Graphs

PBS teams should regularly confirm if they are culturally responsive or if there is over-representation of certain groups of students receiving ODRs. Groups of students could be racial/ethnic groups, special needs students, LGBTQ students, socio-economic status or other groups. This is known as disproportionate discipline and is very common in schools across the nation. This problem can be corrected.

Over-representation could indicate inequitable discipline policies or practices. This may be due to systemic bias, inequitable enforcement of a school's 4-part Accountability System or inadequate teaching of the Accountability System.

We would expect the percent of ODRs for any group to be about the same as their population in the school. A 10% or greater difference indicates over-representation of ODRs.

Calculate disproportionality with two data points:

1. # Students in Group A / Total Students X 100
   90 / 500 x 100 = 18%

2. # ODR for Group A / Total ODR X 100
   60 / 200 x 100 = 30%

In the above example, we would expect that since students in Group A make-up about 18% of the school, that they would receive about 18% of the ODRs. However, they received 30% of the ODRs. Group A is over-represented by 12% which could indicate a problem with the discipline system.

Reflection

Take a minute to reflect on the importance of graphing data.
What are some advantages of looking at graphed data?
Which graphs are you most interested in analysing?

Analyse Data Monthly

Now that we have an understanding of the different behaviour data graphs available, let's focus on systematically analysing monthly data to make decisions and solve problems efficiently and effectively.

Data Analysis Worksheet

Use the Data Analysis Worksheet to make your job of tracking the Big 7 and analysing trends and patterns at your school easier. This worksheet should be completed by your PBS team monthly and then shared with your staff (more about data sharing in the next section). See Figure for worksheet.

The Data Analysis Worksheet tracks the following trends:
- Average Referral and Referral Rate - compare this month to last month and compare with national averages
- Big 7 - who/what/when/where ODRs are happening at school
- Triangle Data - identify the number of students needing additional behaviour support programs, interventions and services
- Suspensions - high numbers mean this isn't an effective consequence because students keep misbehaving
- Absences - high numbers impact learning and achievement
- Tardies - high numbers impact teaching and class climate

Figure 10.2 Data Analysis Worksheet

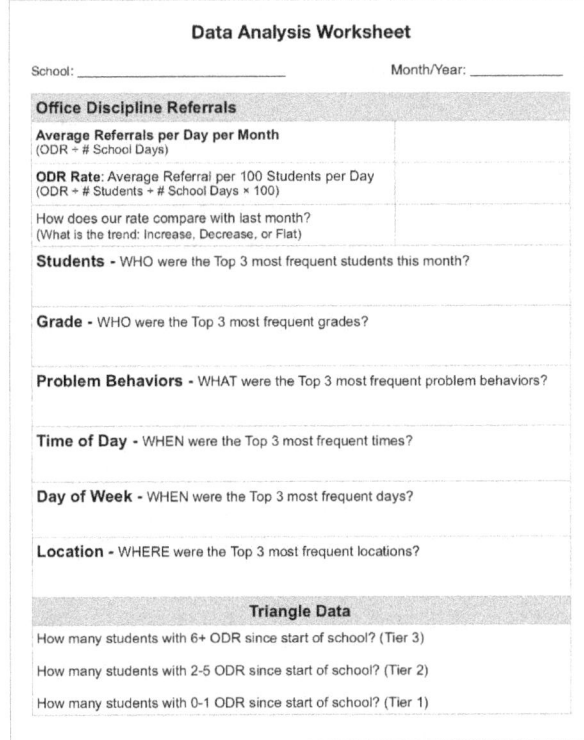
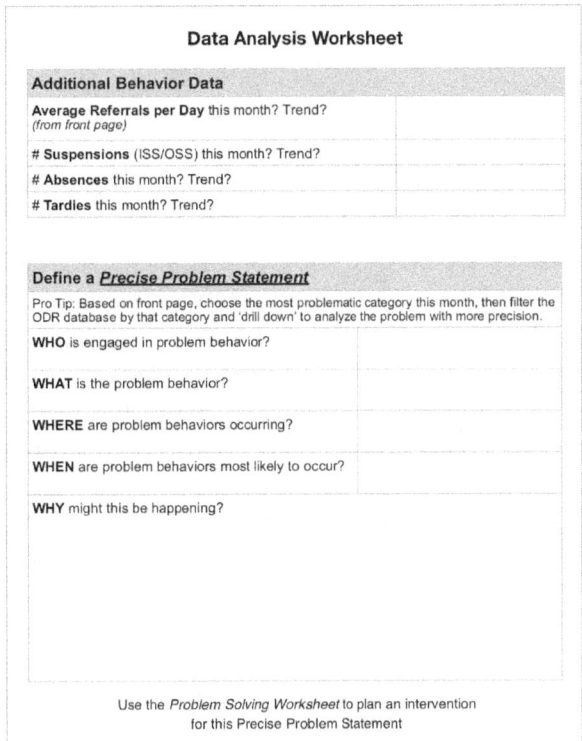

Use your Big 7 data graphs to answer the ODR data questions on the worksheet in about 1-2 minutes. Then the analysis can begin. This is where decision-making and problem-solving happen.

Precise Problem Statement

Too often, teams look at their Big 7 Graphs and only generate Primary Statements. Primary statements are vague and may only consider data from one or two graphs.

Examples of Primary Statements:
- There were too many referrals this month.
- The cafeteria is out of control at lunch.
- Disrespect and referrals for electronics are off the charts.

Decision-making and problem-solving require Precise Problem Statements. Precise problem statements include the five core "W" questions:
Who is engaged in the behaviour?
What is the problem, and how often is it happening?
When is the problem most likely?
Where is it happening?
Why is the problem sustaining?

Example of Precise Problem Statement:
- Tim is hitting peers during lunch in the cafeteria, and his hitting is maintained by peer attention.
- Who-Tim, What-hitting, When-lunch, Where-cafeteria, Why-peer attention

Drill Down into the Data Analysis Worksheet to identify the precise problem statement that your team will solve each month.

Drilling Down into the Data Analysis Worksheet

Drilling Down into the Data Analysis Worksheet allows teams to identify the precise problem statement. All it takes is a few extra steps:
1. Choose one of the top three issues from any of the Big 7 data questions that the team feels is a priority.- Disrespect (What)
2. Filter (sort) the data using that item.- Who/When/Where
3. List the top result for the other items.- 5th grade/1pm after lunch/classroom
4. Discuss possible reasons Why. - Grade 5 students are disrespectful at 1 pm after lunch in the classroom because...chaotic lunchroom climate, returning to class upset, nearing the end of the day, math period (difficult).

Now that the team has a precise problem based on analysing the monthly data a plan to prevent this specific problem can be discussed. The team will need to create an action plan to implement their solution and then review the data in a few weeks to see if their plan solved the problem by drilling down into the data once again.

But none of this would be possible without staff implementing a 4-part accountability system consistently, or students being taught the expectations and reinforced when they get it right.

Common Plans to Prevent Precise Problems

Here are several suggestions that may respond to precise problem statements:
- Reteach expectations or increase reinforcement of a specific problem behaviour
- Reteach expectations or increase reinforcement of specific students
- Reteach expectations or increase reinforcement in a specific location
- Reteach expectations or increase reinforcement at a specific time during the day
- Reteach expectations or increase reinforcement on specific days of the week (after long weekends or holidays)

Share Data Monthly

There are a number of reasons to share school data regularly.

Share data so that staff:
- Know which behaviour interventions are working and which are not
- Feel that collecting data is valuable and worthwhile
- Continue (or start) to implement the school-wide PBS system with fidelity

Sharing data should not be confined to staff meetings. Review the dissemination strategies discussed in the Ownership chapter for ideas on sharing ODR data on a regular basis.

See Gallery for some examples of Data Walls for sharing academic and behaviour data with all staff.

Reflection

Take a minute to reflect on current data sharing practices at your school. Identify the barriers to sharing data regularly...and come up with some solutions.

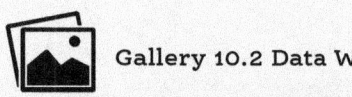 Gallery 10.2 Data Wall

Reading data - SkyView Elementary, Peoria USD

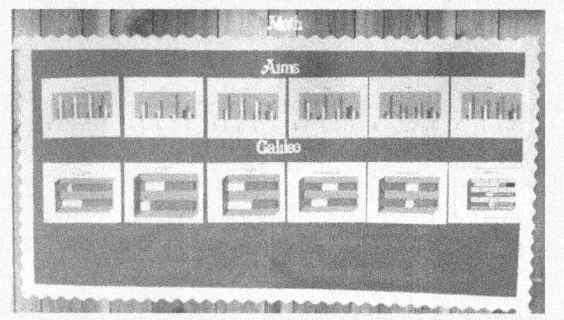
Academic data - Peach Springs Elementary, Hualapai Nation

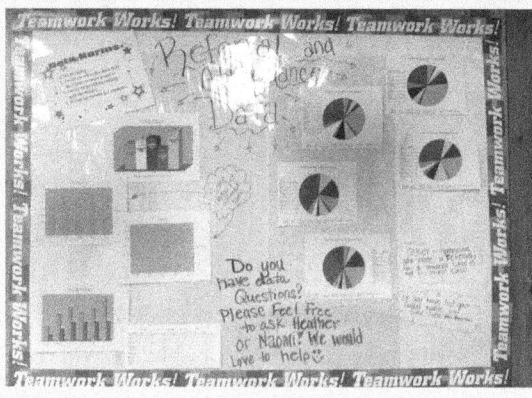
ODR data - Peach Springs Elementary, Hualapai Nation

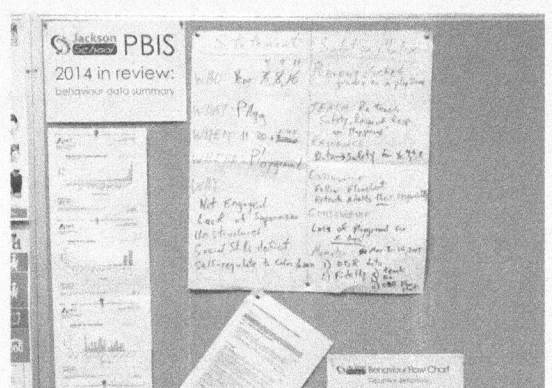
Sharing - Jackson

Action Plan

1. Get access to Big 7 Graphs
2. Get access to Additional Data Graphs
3. Get access to Culturally Responsive data to calculate over-representation or disproportionality of groups of students
4. Complete the Data Analysis Worksheet
5. Set date to share data monthly (at least) with staff

Resources

- Data Analysis Worksheet
- SWIS Comparison Table
- Disproportionality of ODR
- Disproportionality of Suspensions

Available from koi-education.com/resources.

Evaluation

1. The Big 7 data graphs you review monthly should include all of the following except:
   a. Problem Behaviour
   b. Student
   c. Staff
   d. Location
   e. Time of Day
   f. Day of week

2. What is the benefit of using Referral Rate instead of Average Referrals?
   a. Rate reflects the variation in the number of days each month
   b. Rate reflects the variation in the number of students in a school
   c. Rate can be used to compare different schools
   d. All of the above
   e. None of the above

3. According to SWIS Summary data, what is the average amount of ODRs per school day for a high school with 1000 students?
   a. 1207
   b. 12.7
   c. 1.27
   d. 120.7

4. We would expect the percent of ODRs for any group of students to be about the same as their population in the school. A ____% or greater difference indicates over-representation of ODRs.
   a. 5%
   b. 10%
   c. 15%
   d. 20%

5. What is one reason not to share data?
   a. So that staff feel remorse for not being consistent with the PBS reinforcement or accountability system
   b. So that staff know which behaviour interventions are working and which are not
   c. So that staff feel that collecting data is valuable and worthwhile
   d. So that staff continue (or start) to implement the school-wide PBS system with fidelity

Answers: 1c, 2e, 3b, 4b, 5a

THIS PAGE INTENTIONALLY LEFT BLANK

Chapter 11
Roll Out System

YOU CAN DREAM, CREATE, DESIGN, AND BUILD THE MOST WONDERFUL PLACE IN THE WORLD, BUT IT REQUIRES PEOPLE TO MAKE THE DREAM A REALITY.

– WALT DISNEY

Roll Out System

Learning Objectives

Plan a High Energy Kick Off

Organise Multiple Tier 1 PBS Roll Outs

Explore PBS Celebration Ideas

Movie 11.1
Bugs Bunny
Theme Song

View at http://youtu.be/F-t8PngHgWY

Your goal when you Roll Out your PBS system to staff, students, and parents should be to sing the Bugs Bunny theme song with confidence (metaphorically speaking, of course). We will help you prepare for your show!

Overture, curtains, lights,
This is it, the night of nights
No more rehearsing and nursing a part
We know every part by heart.

Overture, curtains, lights
This is it, you'll hit the heights
And oh what heights we'll hit
On with the show this is it!

Preview

You may be asking yourself, "Are we ready for the Roll Out"? Readiness means that all Action Plans are completed and the TIC (Team Implementation Checklist) from PBISapps.org is up to date.

Assess what is completed and 'In Place', then assign people and resources to the 'Not In Place' list to ensure that all the pieces of your puzzle are ready for your grand Roll Out!

Take a look at the PBS Tier 1 graphic to refresh your memory on everything you've created and give yourself a round of applause!

Figure 11.1 KOI PBS Tier 1

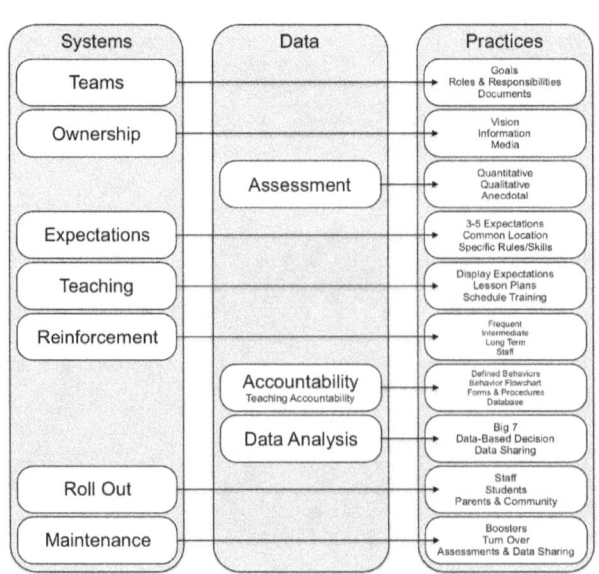

PBIS Tier 1 Manual

Artefacts of PBS

At the end of each chapter in the KOI PBS Tier 1 Manual, an Action Plan was included listing 'To Do' tasks to help schools organise and assign items required for a PBS system.

Now, we have an additional tool called the Artefact Checklist that identifies all the products or physical artefacts required to Roll Out the PBS system. Take a moment to complete this checklist to ensure you have all the documents, posters, lesson plans and matrices needed.

Gallery 11.1
Artefact Checklist

Artifact Checklist

School Name: _____ District: _____

Use this checklist to assess PBIS Tier 1 artifacts and permanent products

System	Check when Complete
Team	
Team Charter (Record of team members, roles, vision/goals, decision making process, norms and meeting times)	
Working Smarter Matrix - audit of all school teams/committees	
Staff Ownership	
Share Who/What/When/Why information about PBIS	
Awareness campaign via meetings/print/web/social/myPBIS.org	
Assessment System	
Team Survey (3x) - Tiered Fidelity Inventory (TFI) in PBISapps	
Staff Survey (1x) - Self-Assessment Survey (SAS) in PBISapps * recommended for teams already implementing some Tier 1 practices	
KOI Climate Surveys (1x) - for staff, students, parents on koi-education.com/resources page	
Expectation System	
Expectation Matrix (School-wide expectations and rules/skills)	
Expectation Posters for each school location (include rules/skills)	
Teaching System	
Lesson Plans to teach each Expectation in each location to students	
Schedule training to teach expectations to staff and students * schedule for first week of school during annual Kick-Off/Roll-Out	
Reinforcement System	
Reinforcement Matrix (4-part system)	
Reinforcement tickets, certificates, menu of reward choices, etc.	
Lesson Plan to teach reinforcement to students (during annual Kick-Off/Roll-Out)	
Accountability System	
Behavior Flowchart & Defined Behaviors	
Office Discipline Referral Form (ODR, 9 items)	
ODR Paper Handling Procedures	
Database to enter ODR's and easily graph ODR by rate/month, problem behaviors, student, grade, location, time, day, motivation	
Lesson Plan to teach accountability to students (during annual Kick-Off/Roll-Out)	
Case Study ppt to teach accountability system to staff	
Roll Out	
Plan to Roll Out/Kick-Off PBIS system to Staff, Students, Parents and Community (during annual Kick-Off/Roll-Out)	
Maintenance	
PBIS digital-Folder/Binder	
PBIS Staff Handbook	

Plan a High Energy Kick-Off

What is a PBS Kick-Off?

The Kick-off is a high profile way to introduce students to PBS and let them know what will happen this year. The purpose is to get students excited about your expectations and a new positive school climate!

Research has shown that adding a "Kick-Off" to your PBS activities increases the likelihood of sustainability" (Muscott & Mann, 2004).

Goals of the Student Kick-Off:

1. Share your PBS Vision.
"This year, we are going to work together to build a positive culture in our school. We want students to interact with each other with respect, and adults to also interact with students using respect. Today, we are going to teach you what is expected of you here at school AND we are going to tell you what you can expect from us. We are going to celebrate regularly when students meet the school-wide expectations, chosen by you, and we are going to point out when students are not meeting our expectations so we can re-teach them to you."

2. Announce that you will build a positive school culture with your school-wide Expectations
"Thanks to the staff and student body and our vote last spring, we have three PRIDE Expectations. These will be posted in all locations of the school along with the PRIDE rules."

3. Announce that expected behaviours will be acknowledged
"When staff see you meeting the PRIDE Expectations by demonstrating one of the PRIDE rules, staff will give you a PRIDE Ticket. Tickets will be drawn from the PRIDE Locker in the library weekly, monthly, and quarterly for additional student recognition awards and privileges."

4. Announce that problem behaviours will be corrected
"When students do not meet the PRIDE Expectations on campus, staff will follow the interventions on the Behaviour Flowchart. The Flowchart is posted in every class and shows the steps that will be taken every time by every staff for every student who chooses to disrupt the learning of others."

This Student Kick-Off is then followed by the Student Roll Out where the actual "teaching" occurs. Review the Teaching System for ideas, plans, and strategies.

The goal of a PBS Kick-Off is not to teach the PBS system, but to introduce it and celebrate it!

Planning the Kick-Off

The Kick-Off must occur at the beginning of the school year, typically the first day of school. Plan activities, plan your music selection and discuss how to best introduce the new PBS system in a fun and engaging way. Have fun with it!

Consider asking your technology or media specialist, arts or music teachers, or student organisations to help organise the Kick-Off events and festivities. Parent associations are also great allies for funding Kick-Off event materials.

Let's take a look at some fun examples!

Movie 11.2 Powell Middle School
Kick-Off During a Student Assembly, http://youtu.be/ZYfwtws9X7k

Movie 11.3 Hillcrest Elementary
Principals broadcasting a Kick-Off, http://youtu.be/BOEHEK9aEOo

Movie 11.4 Zimmerman Elementary
A whole-school music video showcasing Kick-Off week and a great school climate and culture, http://youtu.be/jhEjycWp1uk

Tips:
- To ensure students notice a physical difference around school and not just a procedural one when they arrive on campus, have all Expectation posters ready to hang before or during your Kick-Off.
- A new look on campus creates a new attitude and a feeling that anything (positive) is possible this year!

Reflection

*Take one minute to anticipate possible challenges and/or barriers to the PBS Kick-Off at your school.
How can these challenges be overcome or prevented?*

Organise Multiple Tier 1 PBS System Roll Outs

Kick Offs are a lot of fun! But Roll Outs are where the actual teaching and practice happens. Teaching is critical!

Four Types of Roll Outs Are Necessary to Teach Your PBS System:

1. Staff Roll Out
2. Student Roll Out
3. Parent Roll Out
4. Community Roll Out

Staff Roll Out

The Staff Roll Out will be most successful if you can set aside some time for professional development before the school year begins! The Roll Out for staff (the first year) takes on average about 6 hours - but this should not be in one session.

During the Staff Roll Out, make sure to remind staff of your Vision, your purpose, and goals for implementing PBS? One example of a PBS vision may be, "To empower students to succeed academically and behaviourally". See Ownership System Chapter for a refresher.

Include administrators in planning since many 'hourly' staff are not typically present during the 'teacher training days' prior to students beginning class. This will incur fiscal planning and budgeting.

Include ALL School Staff:
- Teachers
- Paraprofessionals
- Substitutes (will they get Reinforcement Tickets and ODR forms when they check-in at the office?)
- Cafeteria/Crossing Guards/Volunteers
- SLP/OT/PT, EDP or alternative school staff
- Before/After school program staff
- Other…?

Before the School Year Begins, Teach:
1. What is PBS?
    - Show *Creating the Culture of PBS* Video

2. Why is PBS needed here?
    - Share current ODR data
    - Share Climate Survey data again

3. What are the outcomes of PBS?
   - Reduce Behaviour Problems
   - Increase Academic Achievement
   - Improve School Safety and Climate

4. Present all the elements of the Tier 1 PBS System:
   - Expectation Matrix
   - Teaching Lesson Plans
   - Reinforcement Matrix
   - Behaviour Flowchart
   - ODR Form and Procedures

5. Provide staff with PBS Handbook
   - Expectation Matrix
   - Lesson Plans
   - Reinforcement Matrix
   - Tickets
   - Behaviour Flowchart
   - ODR Form
   - Minor Behaviour Tracking Form

6. Ensure that staff can demonstrate using each of the above practices correctly.

7. Share your plans for your student, parent and community Roll Out.

8. Teach staff their Kick-Off responsibilities:
   - Engage all adults in the school to participate in the Student Kick-Off events

Practice

The Staff Roll Out is more than reintroducing PBS and sharing the good news that the system is complete and ready to Roll Out. It is about teaching all staff to implement the system. Here are some elements to practice:

- Reteach the Expectation Matrix and remind staff why it is necessary
- Introduce the lesson plans and practice teaching the expectations
- Practice reinforcing students with your tickets when expected behaviour is demonstrated - and teach the Reinforcement Matrix so staff know what students are supposed to do with the tickets
- Allow staff to practice giving each other tickets and provide corrective feedback to ensure it's done using the 3-step reinforcement process
- Provide instructional feedback
- Teach the Accountability System, provide case studies and make sure staff understand the Flowchart and forms
- Practice filling out the ODR and Minor Behaviour Tracking Form

The goal of the Staff Roll Out is to make sure all adults in the school know the system, practice using the system and feel competent with the system in order to increase fidelity when the system is Rolled out.

It is important to let staff know who to contact if they have questions or need help during the year when implementing this new PBS system.

Student Roll Out

Before we can expect students to meet our expectations, we need to explicitly TEACH them our school-wide Expectations, Reinforcement, and Accountability Systems.

The Teaching System Chapter in the KOI PBS Tier 1 Manual outlined strategies for teaching students your system elements. Lesson plans and video examples were shared. Review that chapter when planning your Roll Out activities.

Passport Activity or Learning Stations

A popular approach to rolling out PBS at the beginning of the school year is to have classes or groups rotate to the different locations listed on your Expectation Matrix. Students are then taught and can practice demonstrating the expectation skills/rules in the location where they need to be applied.

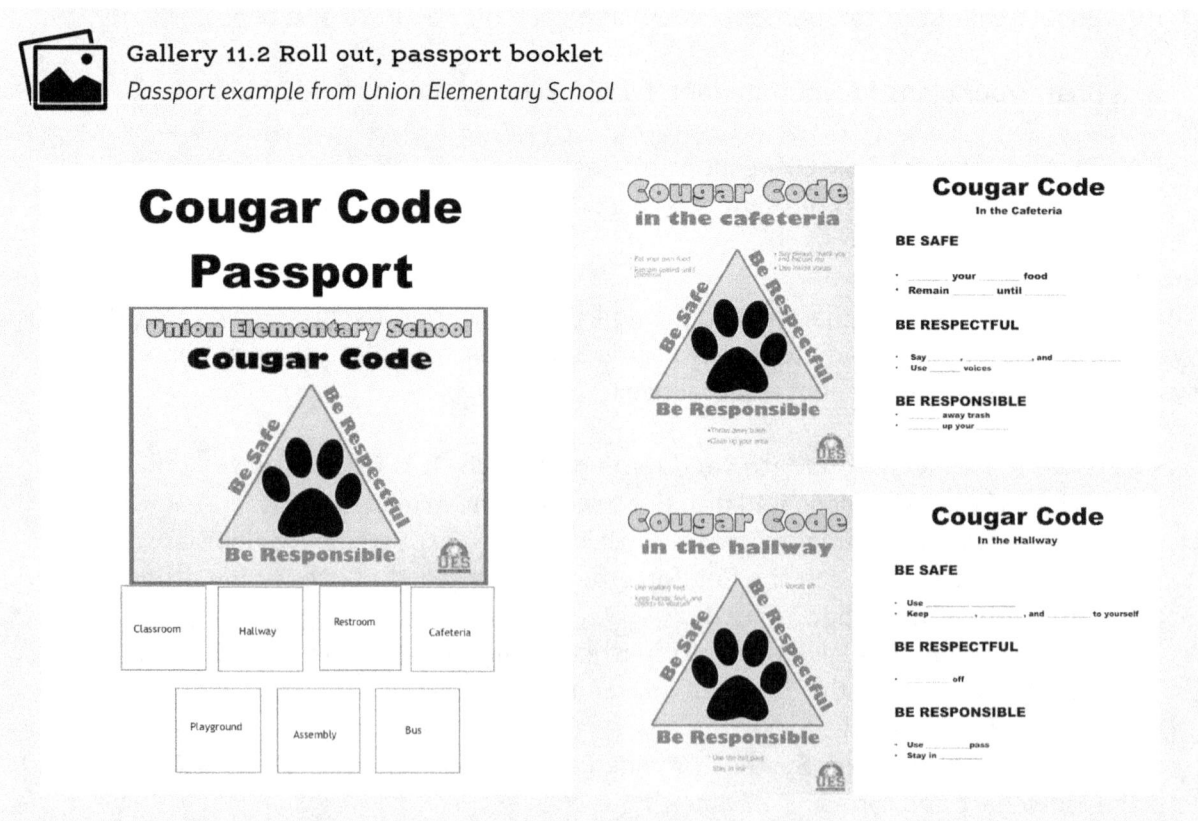

Gallery 11.2 Roll out, passport booklet
Passport example from Union Elementary School

Tips:
- Trained staff or students can be stationed at each location
- Set up a rotation schedule so teachers know when/where to take their students (and attend with them)
- Print Passport style booklets and give students a stamp or sticker for demonstrating the expectation skills at each location

Parent Roll Out

Plan a special Roll Out of your PBS System for parents and community members. Popular examples of communicating your schools Behavioural Expectations and Reinforcement System with parents include:
- Newsletters
- Open House
- Notes home
- School website
- Social media posts, videos and content (review Ownership System Chapter for details)

Community Roll Out

Take advantage of sharing your PBS system with your community and local businesses because it takes a village to raise a child. Some ideas include:
- Press release to your local community paper, radio or TV stations or tweet the regional journalist covering education news
- Post "Community Expectations" in local stores, restaurants, coffee shops, theatres and other shops (with the owner's permission, of course)
- Share reinforcement tickets with store owners and teach them how to use them to acknowledge student demonstrating school Expectations such as 'Respect' in their establishment

> **Reflection**
>
> *Take one minute to discuss why each of the four Roll-Outs are crucial*
> *What other ideas can you think of?*

Explore PBS Celebration Ideas

After the first days of school have come and gone in a blur, be sure to plan for a PBS celebration.

Celebrations typically occur at the end of the first month or first quarter of school. Use them as booster events to reinforce the new school-wide PBS system and celebrate the new positive and proactive ways you have been doing this year.

Some examples of PBS celebrations include:

Elementary	High School
• Game day	• Relaxed dress code
• Picnic	• School spirit day
• Carnival	• Class pride
• Parade	• Club competition
• School spirit dress code	• Festival of nations

Use your imagination - get the whole school, staff, and student body involved. This is a great opportunity to showcase your new system to your community!

Annual Rollout Checklist

Here is an easy list to follow to ensure you have everything ready for your annual PBS Roll Out!

ODR Checklist	
Staff	**Students**
✔ Kick Off	✔ Kick Off
✔ Expectation Matrix & Lesson Plans	✔ Lesson Plans
✔ Reinforcement System & 3-step/3-sec Reinforcement	✔ Reinforcement System
✔ Behaviour Flowchart &Case Study	✔ Behaviour Flowchart
✔ ODR Form	
✔ Minor Behaviour Tracking Form	
✔ Accountability Procedures	

Action Plan

1. Plan a PBS Student Kick-Off
2. Plan a Staff Roll Out
3. Plan a Student Roll Out
4. Plan a Parent Roll Out
5. Plan a Community Roll Out
6. Schedule PBS Celebrations throughout the year

Resources

- Artefacts of PBS
- Action Plans
- Video examples from this chapter

Available from koi-education.com/resources.

Evaluation

1. According to research, why is it important to have a formal Kick- Off?
   a. It is fun
   b. Students like it
   c. It increases the likelihood of sustainability
   d. Teachers like it

2. How many Roll Outs must we plan for?
   a. One
   b. Two
   c. Three
   d. Four

3. It is necessary to Roll Out to the Community:
   a. True
   b. False

Answers: 1c, 2d, 3a

Chapter 12
Maintenance System

COMING TOGETHER IS THE BEGINNING.

KEEPING TOGETHER IS PROGRESS.

WORKING TOGETHER IS SUCCESS.

– HENRY FORD

Maintenance System

> **Learning Objectives**
>
> *Plan Multiple Booster Activities*
>
> *Identify Protective Factors in Staff Turn-Over*
>
> *Schedule Assessments and Data Sharing*

We've known for a long time that learning is a multi-phase process. All learners go through an Acquisition Phase, Fluency Phase, Maintenance Phase, and Generalisation Phase as they acquire and use new knowledge.

This is as true of learning to read, as it is for learning math, piano, driving a car or PBS.

We must plan for the maintenance of our PBS system because it will not sustain by chance and staff will often fall back on old habits. Fortunately, there is a lot of research and evidence to guide us on what works and what doesn't. There is no need to waste time with a trial and error approach to PBS!

Follow the objectives in this chapter to ensure that your PBS system is maintained and sustainable in the face of the constant changes we experience in school.

Preview

Now that your PBS Systems, Data, and Practices are created, and you've rolled it out, it is time to focus on keeping this new system deeply embedded in your school culture.

Boosters are retraining sessions that build on the acquisition phase of learning and promote fluency, maintenance, and generalisation of new skills. Boosters will help ensure your PBS system and the work you have done will last more than one school year.

Plan Multiple Booster Activities

According to Dr. Kent McIntosh, Co-Director of the Center for PBS, researcher have identified four key elements for maintaining and sustaining PBS systems (PBS Leadership Forum, 2009). In addition to teaching and reinforcing the Tier 1 components to students and staff, PBS will be maintained if it is:

1. A Priority
2. Effective
3. Efficient
4. Adaptable

4-Square Activity:

Material: Poster size paper (or blank paper), markers and pens.

1. Draw a large square with four quadrants.
2. Label each square with one of the following key elements to sustaining PBS in schools.
3. After learning about each element, brainstorm ideas and examples of how your team could implement each element at your school.

PBS Sustainability	
Priority	Effective
Efficient	Adaptable

1. Priority

Increase priority by elevating PBS's importance in comparison to other practices, incorporating it into policy, and connecting it to other initiatives. Ways to focus priority:
- Maximise visibility
- Present data to people with resources
- Describe the effects of abandoning support for the practice
- Get it into written policy
- Braid project with other initiatives
- Show how practice can lead to other positive outcomes of new initiatives

Examples:
- Include a diverse group of stakeholders on the PBS team (see Team Chapter)
- Disseminate PBS information regularly using multiple channels (see Ownership System Chapter)
- Publish/schedule PBS activities on a monthly calendar of events (see Teaching System Chapter)
- Schedule weekly/monthly reinforcement blitz (see Reinforcement System Chapter)
- Schedule booster sessions at the beginning of school year and after quarterly/term breaks (see Roll Out System Chapter)

2. Effective

PBS will be perceived as effective if it produces the desired results. School should demonstrate this effectiveness through data sharing with the effects attributed to the practice of PBS. Augment PBS effectiveness through:
- Selecting evidence-based practices that are most likely to produce the desired outcomes (see KOI PBS Tier 2 Manual, Behaviour Screening chapter)
- Assessing fidelity of implementation and retraining when necessary (see Assessment System Chapter)

Examples:
- Share data that shows how implementing PBS can be linked to academic, behavioural, social, and school climate/safety outcomes (see Data Analysis Chapter and data sharing section)
- Share the Big 7 and other data graphs regularly
- Schedule fidelity assessments (See Figure 12.3)
- Reteach/review the core Tier 1 systems: Expectation Matrix, Reinforcement Matrix, and Behaviour Flowchart to staff and students at least annually or biannually

3. Efficient

No one wants "one-more-thing" on their plate. The job of the PBS team is to make PBS easier to implement over time. We must also work to make it easier on resources including both time and money. Enhance PBS efficiency through:
- Collaborating with community partners and donors to support the students and staff acknowledgment and reinforcement system
- Producing durable training products such as videos, slideshows, or training manuals

Examples:
- PBS Team Binder/Electronic Folder (See next objective)
- PBS Staff Handbook (See next objective)
- Print PBS Expectations, Reinforcement, and Accountability System in the student handbook
- Print a small Expectation Matrix and Behaviour Flowchart onto staff ID cards or lanyard
- Post videos on the school or your custom myPBIS.org website demonstrating Expectation examples or How-To deliver Reinforcement Tickets correctly

4. Adaptable

Nothing stays the same for very long. Count on changes in team members, administrators, district initiatives and national or state policies over the years. These changes can derail PBS or make it feel 'old' or something that 'other teachers' did. Maximise PBS adaptability through:
- Using data-based decision making
- Adjusting practices based on changing environments
- Connecting with communities of practice

Examples:
- Attend conferences such as APBS.org, BET-C.org or other regional events
- Continue receiving coaching from an external coach or trainer
- Participate in a Professional Learning Community (PLC) such as #PBISchat on Twitter

Reflection

Take a minute to reflect on your 4-Square List
Which examples/actions are the priority? Why?

Identify Protective Factors in Staff Turn-Over

Change happens. If one person on your PBS team does all the work or there is one Champion in the school or district who 'makes things happen' for PBS, where will you be when that Champion leaves (intentionally or not)? Be prepared for change and staff turn-over by putting three protective factors in place.

1. PBS Team Binder / Electronic Folder

Your PBS Team Binder or digital folder should contain all the team training and planning documents you have produced:
- Team Charter, agendas, minutes, action plans.
- Team training slides, handouts, notes
- PBS products and artefacts

Ideally, teams should have all of these documents in digital format and accessible to all PBS team members - a Cloud Drive is perfect for this.

This KOI PBS Tier 1 Manual should also be kept with the PBS Team Binder since it will have your notes and annotations from the training workshops.

We suggest putting a library bar code on all KOI PBS manuals and Team Binder for staff to sign out from the school library. This way they are returned to the library each year.

See a sample table of contents for a Team Binder/Folder in Figure 12.1.

Figure 12.1 Table of Contents
PBS Team Binder/Folder

Folder or Binder Tab	Contents
Team	• team charter • agenda • minute • working smarter matrix
Action Plans	• Action plans #1-12
Ownership System	• PBIS Vision • PBIS FAQ: what is PBIS?, why is PBIS needed here?, what are PBIS outcomes? • Content for your myPBIS.org website
Assessment	• Data Audit Tool (annual) • Climate data (annual) • PBISapps Assessment fidelity survey graphs • Assessment Matrix • Intervention Matrix • SRSS-IE spreadsheet
Expectation System	• Expectation Matrix • Expectation Posters
Teaching System	• Lesson Plans for each Expectation in each Location
Reinforcement System	• Reinforcement Matrix • Reinforcement Tickets • Reinforcement Certificate
Accountability System	• Behavior Flowchart • Lesson Plan to teach Behavior Flowchart to students • Case Study ppt for Teaching Accountability to staff • Minor Behavior Tracking Form • ODR Form • ODR Paper Handling Procedures
Data System	• Data Analysis Worksheet (monthly) • Problem Solving Worksheet (monthly)
Roll Out System	• Staff Kick Off slides • Student Kick Off slides • Staff Roll Out Schedule • Student Roll Out Schedule • Parent/Community Roll Out Schedule
Maintenance System	• PBIS Staff Handbook (for staff, substitute teachers, before/after care staff, OT/PT/SLP, volunteers, etc)

2. PBS Staff Handbook

Sometimes, all staff may not be present at your annual PBS Kick-Off or Roll Out. New staff may be hired mid-year and substitute teachers or casual relief teachers and support staff are often not paid to attend school Professional Development or Professional Learning Committee (PLC) training workshops.

All staff need a quick PBS reference guide to remind them:
- What is PBS and why is it needed here?
- Who can I ask for help on the PBS team?
- What is the expectation matrix and how do I use it?
- What do I say when I hand out reinforcement tickets?
- How do I use the behaviour flowchart when students misbehave?

See a table of contents for a PBS Staff Handbook in Figure 12.2.

Review several school examples at koi-education.com/resources.

Figure 12.2 Table of Contents - PBS Staff Handbook

PBIS Staff Handbook

Table of Contents

Tab	Content
PBIS Introduction	- What is PBIS - Why is it needed here - What are the outcomes
PBIS Team	- PBIS Team members - Meeting dates & times - Contact person
Expectation System	- Expectation Matrix - How to use the expectation system
Teaching System	- Lesson Plans & teaching schedule - How and when to use the lesson plans
Reinforcement System	- Reinforcement Matrix - How to use the reinforcement system
Accountability System	- Behavior Flow Chart, Defined Behaviors List, ODR Forms, ODR Procedures - How to use the flow chart to hold students accountable when they do not meet school-wide expectations
Data Sharing	- Graphs of Big 7 - Data from previous years showing cumulative growth and outcomes for decreased behavior disruptions, increased academic achievement, and improved school safety and climate
Forms	- Reinforcement tickets - Weekly certificates - Monthly/Semester Awards
Notes	-

3. PBS Poster Showcase

A PBS poster showcase is a typical way to show off your PBS Systems, Data, and Practices to staff, students, and parents.

It should be displayed in a conspicuous and prestigious location at your school. It can illustrate the components of your system to substitute teachers, community members or school board members to increasing visibility, priority, and of course to showcase your success! See next Gallery for examples.

Here are examples of artefacts to include:

Systems
Expectation Matrix, Reinforcement Matrix, Behaviour Flowchart, PBS Staff Handbook

Data
Fidelity Assessment (TFI, TIC, BOQ, SET), Climate Surveys, ODR data, other data graphs

Practices
Expectation posters, reinforcement tickets, ODR or MBTF form, print media, photos, videos, social media, or more!

The International Association for Positive Behavior Support (and other education conferences) often encourage schools to submit proposals to showcase their school practices at a Poster Session: APBS.org

Gallery 12.1 Poster Showcase Examples

Schedule Assessment and Data Sharing

Plan to share your data and self-assess PBS fidelity on a regular schedule to promote maintenance of Tier 1 systems and practices.

Assessment Schedule

Our PBS Assessment Schedule (see next Figure) provides a list of several PBS assessments and provides suggestions of when each tool should be completed. Not all Assessment needs to be completed every year. Work with your PBS trainer and coach to make a schedule based on your needs. See the Assessment System Chapter for a review of the Tier 1 PBS assessments.

Surveys to assess the fidelity of Tier 2 and Tier 3 systems are taught in the KOI PBS Tier 2 and Tier 3 Manual. We recommend a robust and effective Tier 1 system before rushing forward with more effort.

Figure 12.3 PBS Assessment Schedule

			Assessment Schedule					
Purpose	Assessment	Description	Who completes survey?	Month	Open Window	Close Window	Share Data	Where is survey? Link URL
Planning	Discuss annual assessment schedule	Plan the 2020/21 calendar, discuss the importance of using survey results to drive decisions, schedule data sharing	District PBIS Team	May MODIFY FOR YOUR CALENDAR			PBIS PD @ start of school year in Aug	Google Drive
Ownership	Data Audit Tool	Formative evaluation data on annual academic, behavior/discipline, special education outcomes	PBIS Team	Sept				KOI-Education.com/resources Tier 1 Assessment
	Climate Survey's	Annual survey of staff, student, parent perception of school climate, culture and safety	Staff, Students, Parents	Sept				PBISapps.org Team leader or data profiler has login access - post link for staff, students, families
PBIS Fidelity -- Schools	TFI - Tiered Fidelity Inventory (Tier 1, 2 or 3)	The purpose of the School-wide PBIS Tiered Fidelity Inventory is to provide an efficient and valid index of the extent to which PBIS core feature are in place withing a school. Tier 1, 2, and 3 sections.	PBIS Team & Coach	Quarterly until 70% fidelity, then Annually				PBISapps.org Team leader or data profiler has login access
	SAS - Self-Assessment Survey	The PBIS Self-Assessment Survey (SAS) is used by school staff for annual assessment of effective behavior support systems in their school. The survey examines the status and need for improvement of four behavior support systems: (a) school-wide discipline systems, (b) non-classroom management systems (e.g., cafeteria, hallway, playground), (c) classroom management systems, and (d) systems for individual students engaging in chronic problem behaviors	Staff - classified and certified	January				PBISapps.org Team leader or data profiler has login access and will send SAS link to all staff (certified/classified)
	SET - School-wide Evaluation Tool	Assess Tier 1 implementation fidelity	External Evaluator	May				PBISapps.org Team leader or data profiles has login access to view report
	ISSET - Individual Student Systems Evaluation Tool	Assess Tier 2/3 implementation fidelity	External Evaluator	May				PBISapps.org Team leader or data profiler has login access to view report
-- District	DSFI - District Systems Fidelity Inventory	PBIS Blueprint to plan systematic implementation and sustainabilty over next 3-5 years	District PBIS Team	Quarterly				KOI-Education.com/resources Tier 1 Teams

Data Sharing

In the Data Analysis Chapter we talked about analysing and sharing the Big 7 graphs with your PBS team and school at least once a month. In the KOI PBS Tier 2 Manual we'll share additional procedures for using data for decision-making and identifying which students need Tier 2 and Tier 3 behaviour interventions.

Here are some reasons to share Assessment Data:
1. To inform stakeholders of implementation integrity.
2. To celebrate success and identify current needs.
3. To create an Action Plan to move forward.

Use this handy checklist for a reminder of the purpose of each tool in the Assessment Schedule

Assessment	Description
Data Audit Tool (DAT)	Summative annual record of academic, behavioral, special education and seclusion/restraint data to analyze trends across years
Climate Survey	Qualitative perception of school climate and safety from staff, students, and parents
Tiered Fidelity Inventory (TFI)	Annual self-assessment of the fidelity of multiple-tiers of a PBS system.
Self-Assessment Survey (SAS)	Annual survey of staff perception of implementation fidelity and implementation priority of a Tier 1 PBS systems
School-wide Evaluation Tool (SET)	Annual evaluation (by a trained external evaluator) of the fidelity of a Tier 1 PBS system

Reflection

Take a minute to reflect on the importance of PBS fidelity.

How will you share assessment results with school staff, students, parents, or school board members?

Action Plan

1. Use Boosters to make PBS a Priority, Effective, Efficient, and Adaptable.
2. Prepare for Turn-Over with a PBS Team Binder/Folder, PBS Staff Handbook, and PBS poster showcase.
3. Share data and fidelity assessments to maintain your PBS system.

Resources

- PBS Team Binder - Table of Contents
- PBS Staff Handbook - Table of Contents
- PBS Poster Showcase and School Examples Photos
- Assessment Schedule
- Various Tier 1 fidelity assessments

Available from koi-education.com/resources.

Evaluation

1. Booster sessions can be used to make PBS:
   a. A Priority and Adaptive
   b. Capable and Durable
   c. Effective and Efficient
   d. Proficient and Resilient
   e. A and C
   f. B and D

2. A PBS Handbook is essential for staff because:
   a. Everyone will be at the Roll Out and Kick-Off
   b. Staff turn over is expected in school
   c. PBS is too complicated
   d. Staff need one more thing on their plate

3. A PBS Showcase poster is optional:
   a. True
   b. False

4. What does the self-assessment survey actually assess?
   a. Staff feelings toward students
   b. School climate and culture
   c. PBS team efficiency and effectiveness
   d. All of the above
   e. None of the above

Answers: 1e, 2b, 3a, 4e

Chapter 13
Acknowledgements

MANY HANDS MAKE LIGHT WORK.

– JOHN HEYWOOD (ENGLISH PLAYWRIGHT/POET)

Authors

Daniel Gulchak, Ph.D.
Dr. Gulchak's passion is sharing the good news about bad behaviour to build the capacity of educators and empower students to succeed. An experienced special education teacher, he specialises in school-wide systems change including Positive Behaviour Supports, classroom and behaviour management strategies and leveraging technology to improve student behaviour and academic achievement.

Yadira Flores, Ph.D., NCSP
Dr. Flores leverages her knowledge and experience in schools to share culturally responsive education and behaviour practices to help students prosper. As a nationally certified school psychologist she is an expert in psychological evaluations, bilingual assessments, and evidence-based learning strategies that impact teacher effectiveness and student's health and well-being.

Angel Jannasch-Pennell, Ph.D.
Dr. Jannasch-Pennell is a leader who connects people and projects with meaningful results that impact the future for children and youth. Her broad experience in education comes from working directly to improve the lives of students with emotional and behavioural disorders to writing and directing multi-million dollar national and international research projects for universities, departments of education, and local schools.

Ruth Reynoso, M.Ed.
Ruth Reynoso loves teaching and sharing her knowledge and experiences with students and adults. She is relatable because she draws from her experiences as an Arizona Master classroom teacher, staff developer, and PBS Team Leader to support the systems change that schools must undergo in order to implement PBS with fidelity.

Special Thanks

Matt Rhoton - Cover design, graphic designer, and KOI Education logo and website designer, DesignByPixel.com

Kegan Remington - 1st Edition eBook layout and media integration

Amy Thompson - 1st Edition credits/citations

Anika Bausom - 4th Edition print layout, Cover design for International Edition, AnikaBausom.com

KOI Education Colleagues - All of the trainers, leaders and coaches that partner with us to improve outcomes for students, educators and families teach us so much and we are very thankful that each one of them is in our lives.

Our Organisation

We love to share **K**nowledge that results in positive **O**utcomes and **I**mpacts society (**KOI**).

KOI Education partners with educators and organisations to deliver high quality evidence-based practices and services that result in measurable academic, behavioural, and social achievements in our education community.

Our focus includes Training, Coaching, Evaluation, and Consultation services in:
- School-wide Positive Behaviour Interventions and Support (PBS)
- Bully Prevention and School Safety
- Trauma Informed Care
- Adverse Childhood Experiences (ACES)
- Advanced special education interventions, strategies and classroom behaviour management support
- Educational leadership and systems change initiatives

PBS Training Academy©

We facilitate professional development training to help schools and districts implement KOI training using our PBS Training Academy. Training is available for Tier 1, Tier 2 and Tier 3 systems. We use research-based fidelity assessments and follow high quality professional development standards.

We will work with your schools before, during and after training to help you build the capacity to make PBS/MTSS a sustainable system.

PBS Trainer-Leader-Coach (TLC) Institute©

Become a Certified PBS Trainer-Leader-Coach for you school, district or state by attending our five days of interactive and intensive trainer-of-trainer program. You will learn the skills necessary to be an expert in training, coaching, evaluation and sustainability of multi-tiered systems of support.

Be a part of the emerging global PBS Professional Learning Network and a champion in improving student outcomes through decreased behaviour problems, increased academic achievement and improved school climate and safety for all. You can make a difference with your leadership!

Tier 1 and Tier 2/3 Institutes are available. Training includes KOI PBS Curriculum, online access to slides, trainer agenda, and training handouts, materials and activities for staff.

PBISS - Positive Bus Safety Systems©

Ask about our curriculum for working with school transportation departments to improve the climate and safety on school buses using PBS. All the elements of a school PBS system work on the bus - but given that the context is very different than a classroom, the implementation must be unique. We have a proven model.

For more information on any of our training, visit our website koi-education.com or email info@koi-education.com for details.

Contact Us

We're easy to find, follow, and friend...make a connection today!

- Phone: 480.420.6564
- Website: Koi-Education.com
- Email: info@Koi-Education.com
- Facebook: facebook.com/KoiEducation
- Twitter: twitter.com/KoiEducation
- YouTube: youtube.com/user/KoiEducation

www.ingramcontent.com/pod-product-compliance
Lightning Source LLC
Chambersburg PA
CBHW080838230426
43665CB00021B/2877